The Wolfpen
NOTEBOOKS

The Wolfpen NOTEBOOKS

A Record of Appalachian Life

JAMES STILL

With a Foreword by Eliot Wigginton

THE UNIVERSITY PRESS OF KENTUCKY

Portions of this book originally appeared in *Foxfire* 22, no. 3 (Fall 1988), and are reprinted by permission of Foxfire Fund, Inc. The bibliography is reprinted from *Iron Mountain Review* by permission of William Terrell Cornett and the publisher. "Heritage" is reprinted from *The Wolfpen Poems* by permission of Berea College Press.

Editorial and Sales Offices: Lexington, Kentucky 40508–4008

Library of Congress Cataloging-in-Publication Data

Still, James, 1906-
   The Wolfpen notebooks : a record of Appalachian life / James Still : with a foreword by Eliot Wigginton.
      p.   cm.
   Includes bibliographical references.
   ISBN 0-8131-1741-0 (alk. paper)
   1. Appalachian Region, Southern—Literary collections.
2. Appalachian Region, Southern—Quotations, maxims, etc.
3. Still, James, 1906-   —Notebooks, sketchbooks, etc.
4. Appalachian Region, Southern—Popular culture.
5. Americanisms—Appalachian Region, Southern. I. Title.
PS3537.T5377W59   1991
818'.5209—dc20   90-22978

Appalachia is that somewhat mythical region with no known borders. If such an area exists in terms of geography, such a domain as has shaped the lives and endeavors of men and women from pioneer days to the present and given them an independence and an outlook and a vision such as is often attributed to them, I trust to be understood for imagining the heart of it to be in the hills of Eastern Kentucky where I have lived and feel at home and where I have exercised as much freedom and peace as the world allows.

—James Still

CONTENTS

FOREWORD

James Still tilted precariously in a ladderback chair in George Brosi's Berea, Kentucky, bookstore. He and I had both been involved that day with events on the Berea College campus, and, as always happens after such activities, we had gone to Appalachian Mountain Books to relax, browse, buy books, talk about new projects, and gather news from George about what other Appalachian writers and publishers were up to.

At over eighty years of age, Still, one of the region's best-loved and most skillful writers, had new projects on his mind. There were unfinished stories to polish, and negotiations to conduct with publishers who might be interested in reprinting some of his work that was now out of print. And lately he had been thinking about a collection of some forty years' worth of sayings and expressions and superstitions he had heard his mountain neighbors use. He had written down all of this material and had squirreled it away in notebooks among the piles of novels and manuscripts and papers in his log house on little Carr Creek. Should he dig those out and take a look at what he had? Might they be worth printing? Would Foxfire's infant book publishing venture be interested?

As an English teacher whose high school students have been collecting such material since 1966 from the North Georgia mountains for our *Foxfire* magazine, I was instantly intrigued. We were not the right publisher, however, being so new to the book business that we had virtually no distribution capability. For him to sign on with us would be economic suicide.

I wanted to be involved, however, for several reasons. Foremost among them was the fact that I was constantly searching for ways to have my students actively involved in some capacity with living authors as an antidote to the old educational paradigm by which public school students are simply driven like mules through books by anonymous authors, one relentless chapter after another, each followed by a mindless quiz designed to "check up on them" to make sure they had carried out the day's assignment. That's the way I had been taught, and even today, as I read, the possibility that I will be quizzed whispers away in the back of my mind.

And so we hammered together a compromise. I would take on the search for a publisher for the sayings. Still would type them up and send them to Rabun County where my students would organize them into appropriate categories and prepare a finished manuscript for his approval. In addition, he agreed to submit to several lengthy tape-recorded interviews by those students about his writing in general and the collection of the sayings in particular—an interview that would become part of the final book to set the sayings in context. In advance of the book's publication, we would produce an issue of *Foxfire* completely devoted to the interview and selections from the manuscript, chosen by the students for our readers.

Several months later, Still visited Rabun County. Two of my classes were ready for him, having devoured *River of Earth*, his most enduring piece of work, and several of his short stories. They interviewed him for nearly three hours in class. Realizing that the students were genuinely interested in the project, he began to type up and send them examples from the unpublished notebooks. The students became more and more intrigued. With the initial interview transcribed and organized, and the photographs the students had taken printed, I took a van load of the most interested ones to the Hindman Settlement School to interview him a second time. By now, Laura Lee, one of the seniors, had volunteered to take primary responsibility for the work, not only editing the best of the interview material but also receiving each new shipment of sayings from Still, organizing them, and typing them into a word processor with the help of other students.

Month by month, as explained by Laura in the following Introduction, the project grew. Still, ever the meticulous author, took the interview material through half a dozen drafts. Just when we thought we had received the final manila envelope full of notebook excerpts, another would arrive with an apologetic, "I just found these and thought we ought to include them." Laura continued her work on the project as a summer job with us. Negotiations with the University Press of Kentucky resulted in a contract with Still to publish the entire manuscript. The issue of *Foxfire* announcing that fact, and devoted to this collaboration, was printed in the fall of 1988.

Meanwhile, nearly a hundred students have been involved in one way or another with this book, and, as an English teacher, I have to believe that their special, unique partnership with James Still has been a far more rewarding experience than some of those I had as a student. And Still himself has been so pleased at the amount of time and energy and genuine interest the students have devoted to the project that he now visits classrooms in Kentucky regularly both to be interviewed and to share his work. For everyone involved, it's been a win-win situation.

And the next time I'm in Appalachian Mountain Books visiting with George and a couple of authors, I'll be watching, fingers crossed, for a similar opportunity to present itself.

Eliot Wigginton

INTRODUCTION   *Laura Lee*

A group of high school students from Rabun County, Georgia, conducted two interviews with James Still, one in our classroom and one in Hindman, Kentucky, where Still lives. Still looks closer to being sixty years young than eighty years old. Although he moves carefully, all his actions are sharp and enthusiastic. He is very expressive in using his hands and changing his facial features to emphasize a point he is making. His face is plump and cheerful, the forehead creased with years stretching back into a smooth, bald head ringed by short white hair. His ears are those of an elf, slightly pointed on the ends. The eyes sometimes seem sad, but they are active, flitting from face to face and giving us each bright, keen glances as he answered our questions. His eyebrows, arched and thickened on the outer edges, give the impression that he is constantly surprised or questioning.

There is nothing artificial about Still. At the outset of the classroom interview, he appeared slightly nervous but answered our questions in a very earnest, straightforward manner. His hands were constantly moving—as if he were telling a story each time he spoke. At one point he described how he created and developed the short story "The Nest." In the tale, a young girl is sent to spend the night with her aunt who lives on the other side of a ridge. It is very cold, and by nightfall the girl is hopelessly lost. The simple plot belies the magnitude of emotion that went into the writing of the tale; although all the elements of the story—plot, theme, vocabulary—are unembellished and straightforward, Still manages to impart a profound sense of sorrow. As he told us how he felt while he was writing "The Nest," his voice became softer, his eyes began to mist, and the eloquent motions of his hands ceased. It was a far better and more lasting example of the strength and meaning of literature than any textbook explanation.

After we completed the interview and Still returned to Kentucky, we discovered that more questions arose from the material we had gathered. We scheduled a second interview to be conducted at the Hindman Settlement School, where Still was employed as the librarian during the Depression. His house is a few miles away and he remains closely associated with the school.

Eight of us decided to make the trip. Our journey to Hindman was not a smooth one by any means. Riding around and over the mountains there was like riding a roller coaster. We drove into Hindman late on a dreary afternoon. Winter mists clung to the sides and floors of hollows, and a light drizzle was just beginning. The mountains around Hindman are steep and bunched tightly together, leaving little space in the winding valleys for any centralized town. There is so little room in the valley that to fit in the creek, highway, and string of houses, rock had been cut away from the mountain. "Cutting away that mountainside made this town twice its size," Still told us later.

We stayed overnight at the Hindman Settlement School. After breakfast in the morning, James Still joined us in the kitchen while we were cleaning up the dishes we had used. We began the interview in the school's dining room. This second interview was much more detailed than the first; not only did he answer some in-depth questions concerning his writing but he also shared with us his views on education and politics. He had brought with him some of the twenty-three spiral notebooks in which he had recorded expressions and phrases people used that caught his attention and seemed worth writing down. Sometimes it would be an exchange of only a few words between two people; other times he would hear reminiscences of past events or full-fledged accounts of local history. These were tidbits that came about through the natural course of conversation; he heard statements that might never have been

"Any writer of merit I know is constantly trying to find the time and the place to sit at his typewriter and indulge himself."

shared in a tape recorded interview. Still would make a mental note of these conversational excerpts or jot them down immediately on any available scrap of paper, and later record them in one of the spiral-bound notebooks he used especially for this purpose. On occasion, he would have the opportunity to use some of these excerpts in his writing, since the characters and locations that make up his stories are of the same region from which he collected the contents of the notebooks.

After the interview, Wig visited with Mike Mullins, the director of the school, and the rest of us dispersed into little groups to walk around until it was time for lunch. Still asked if we would like him to give us a ride into town. Suzie Nixon, Darren Volk, and I piled into his Chrysler Le Baron and he drove us into Hindman. He was full of stories and jokes. "See that sign over there?" he asked, pointing to the sign at the entrance to the school, commemorating its founding. "That's the most enduring of my writings."

While Still went into the post office, we waited in his car. In the front seat, a wilting red carnation reposed on top of a pile of multicolored, woven floor mats and assorted sales papers. In the back seat, we noticed tapes of Schubert, Kenny Rogers, and Gregorian chants. From the variety in his musical taste, we ascertained that he must be a person with complex interests. This was not in keeping with our view of his simple writing method or the overall uncomplicated image he portrayed, however. We decided there was really no way we could slide his character into a single, neatly analyzed slot. Later, though, he unconsciously helped us solve some of the mystery of his personality. "There are two different types of people," he told us. "Primary people don't think about *not* saying hello to you and secondary people wait till you say hello first—a type of inverted ego, you know." It appeared to us that Still belonged to the "primary" category.

We returned to the school for lunch. Many members of the staff were there, and several toddlers were seated at a table next to us. At one point, a small boy who had been standing on his chair—much to the chagrin of his mother—toppled to the floor. Silence enveloped the dining room for a tense moment until the child, unabashed, resumed his chair to finish eating. When we expressed our concern, Still smiled. "Oh, he does that every day! I was waiting for him to do that. Now I can relax and eat my meal in peace!"

Although Still now lives inside the city limits of Hindman, he also owns a log house between Dead Mare Branch and Wolf Pen Creek on Little Carr Creek. It was willed to him by Jethro Amburgey, a well-known woodscraftsman and dulcimer maker, while Still was a librarian at Hindman. It was during one summer while he was living in the log house that he composed his first novel. *River of Earth* was published in 1940 and is still in print today. It is his most enduring work.

When James Still wants to get away to a quiet place to write, he goes to the two-room house on Little Carr Creek. It is constructed of gray, hewed logs and has two windows on the bottom floor. As we got out of the van and walked toward the house, we noticed two small plank buildings on the right of the path, both weathered gray. The first was an outdoor toilet and the second was a storage building. We were curious so we looked inside the outhouse. Hanging on the left were several corn cobs in a glass case. Below the case was a sign that read, "In case of emergency, break glass."

Scattered through the trees from the gate to the log house were aluminum pot pie pans with the bottoms up. Stuck through the bottoms were Christmas lights. At night, these lighted a walkway from the gate to his house. About forty-five feet from the front door was a water well. Jim Amburgey once said, "I've been coming to this house since I was a child. I come here for a good drink of water. This is the best well in the country."

Hanging on the side of the log house at the back door was a beat-up washpan. Still said the washpan had been used in the movie "Coal Miner's Daughter" and was left behind. Below the washpan was a sign made of tin with Still's name on it. Above the door was a horseshoe.

The air smelled like cut grass, and everything was wet from an earlier rain. We could hear the birds singing and the water dripping from the trees. "In spring," Still commented, contemplating the barren flower beds, "there are some fifty varieties of daffodils in bloom here."

He led us through the back door into a small kitchen where two cats were asleep on the weathered tile floor. From there we entered the main room of the house. In one corner was a bed with a nightstand by its head. On the table was a modern telephone, and hanging on the wall above it was an old crank phone. In the opposite corner stood a bureau and mirror with old photographs and other memorabilia, and next to that, positioned in front of an unused fireplace, was a gas heater that Still turned on to take the chill out of the damp air when we entered the

"The log house
I moved into
was built in
1827. . . . I had
found a home."

Right, floor-
plan of James
Still's log house.

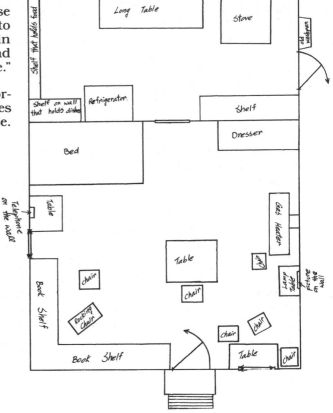

house. At the far end of the room, a bookcase containing old magazines and novels, such as *The Grapes of Wrath*, occupied one corner; in the other was a ladder attached to the wall, leading to the attic room. In the wall between these two corners was the front door, facing directly the door to the kitchen. In the center of the room, a rocking chair had been pulled up to a table strewn with papers and books.

Still would bring our attention to an object in the room, tell us what it was, where and when it had come into his possession, and what was special about it. Then he would ask us to take notice of something else, keeping us so busy with anecdotes that we hardly needed to ask questions. After we had satisfied our curiosity about his house and were settling comfortably into chairs or on the bed, Still searched through the papers on the center table until his hands closed around an aged issue of *Esquire*. Standing with his back to the heater, he extracted a pair of reading glasses from his breast pocket and proceeded to read aloud "Dance on Pushback Mountain," a poem of his that appeared in the October 1936 issue. He spoke in a very straightforward and natural manner, as if he were remembering a conversation he had heard recently rather than reading print. His voice added a new dimension to the words that we would have missed had we been reading them silently to ourselves.

One thing Still was worried about when he first considered allowing us to print quotations from his notebooks was that spoken words lose a certain value when written. The tone of the narrator's voice, his inflections, his hands and facial expressions all combine to give greater meaning and substance to words. Just by changing inflections, two totally different tales can be made. Still pointed out, for example, how one tale could be told, changing inflections on only one syllable to give it two radically different endings: "The two towns of Sassafras and Vicco were growing so rapidly that their edges nearly touched. The town councils met together to decide if the two towns should merge or not. After the decision had been made, a citizen of Vicco stood up to deliver his opinion. 'Goodbye, God. We're moving to Sassafras!' " Whereas the real story ended: "Good, by God. We're moving to Sassafras!"

A second reservation came from his concern that the majority of the notebook excerpts are not flashy or sensational but are rather homespun, quiet images of his community. He realized the value of the material, but was it material that needed to be published? In addition, he was concerned that many of the excerpts depended on the mood of the moment or the context of the conversation to be appreciated thoroughly.

In the end, however, he decided that this material deserved to be in print. After we returned home, he began the selection process, and every few weeks a manila envelope would arrive in Georgia containing another collection of pages filled with the sayings, typed and double-spaced, for us to divide up into categories, retype, and arrange. The process lasted for months.

To the very last, we could only guess at the reason Still decided, finally, to allow this material to be published. On one of the last pages he sent us, he provided the answer himself: "The first notebook entry was recorded some forty-five years ago. Most of the participants are dead. Save for their gravestones, this is the only record for some that they lived and laughed and wept and had opinions like the rest of us. I have long tried to speak for them. Here they are speaking for themselves." This book is the result of Still's decision to publish.

INTERVIEW   *Laura Lee*

"This fellow has come over in here from Troublesome
Creek and settled in the Old Wiley Amburgey house on
Dead Mare Branch and we hain't learnt his name yet, or
what's in his head. We call him 'the man in the bushes.' "
[1939]

My paternal grandparents were William Watson Still and
Annie McClendon Still, and my mother's parents were
James Benjamin Franklin Lindsey and Carrie Jackson
Lindsey. My forebears from both sides first settled in Virginia during pioneer days. The Lindseys set down near
Berryville and the Stills in what is now Lee County near
Jonesville. There's a roadside marker at Jonesville noting
the birthplace of Alfred Taylor Still,[1] the man who con-
ceived the medical system of osteopathy. Jonesville is up
the road from Cumberland Gap where I came to attend college in 1924. I didn't know then I was completing a genea-
logical circle. We've figured that my ancestors fought in the
American Revolution and that frontier land was allotted
them as reward for their services. The Lindseys in Georgia,
the Stills in Alabama. And not many miles apart.
    My mother, Lonie Lindsey Still, grew up on a farm near
Franklin, Georgia. Her mother, my grandma, had been
married before to a Civil War soldier who lost his life in
the struggle to head off Sherman in the march toward Atlanta. Grandpa was an orphan, three years younger than

1. He is of the same "set" of Stills but the exact relationship is
not known.

Grandma, and having never seen his father could cure thrush in children.[2] Uncle Edd told me that during my mother's childhood the floor of their Georgia home where the cookstove was was beaten earth. The move to Alabama, some three miles from the Stills, may have been spurred by the destruction of the home by a cyclone. Beforehand, Grandpa mined enough gold on his land to fill his teeth.

Grandpa Still fought in the Civil War and suffered a wound to the body and had a finger shot off by a Yankee bullet. I recall his discussing with a comrade the mining of the Confederate trenches by the North at Petersburg toward the end of the conflict. He regularly attended Old Soldiers' conventions in Richmond, Montgomery, New Orleans, or wherever held.

There were ten of us children, five girls and five boys. The sisters came first. I am the eldest son and the only surviving member of the family. When my parents first married, they homesteaded in Texas in 1893, and two children were born there. I would have been born in Texas had my parents not come to Alabama on a visit and one of my little sisters died of scarlet fever. Just before she died she asked my mother not to leave her, and so Mama never would go back to Texas and leave her grave. The cotton farm Papa cultivated is now a part of the Fort Hood reservation and I suppose is regularly plowed by tanks and heavy artillery.

I was born in 1906 on Double Branch farm just outside of LaFayette. Sometimes I tell people I was born in a cotton patch. Anyhow, I came to consciousness there. One of my first memories is of running about with a small sack on my back Mama had sewed up for me. I'd pick a boll here and yonder and everywhere. Along about the time I was eight I took on the job of milking the cow. I recollect going out barefoot on cold mornings and the cow stepping on my foot. Before starting to milk into the bucket I'd scoot a stream into my mouth, and a couple into the cat's mouth.

2. Grandpa's father died before Grandpa was born. Having never seen his father, Grandpa had the gift, according to folk wisdom, of curing thrush in children. He accomplished this by blowing his breath into the child's mouth. Grandpa's mother's family name was Lanier—of the Georgia Laniers.

My mother was a worker. She had to be in order to raise ten children, to cook, to make most of our clothes, to do the laundry and ironing, the canning and preserving and keeping house. Besides this, she quilted and crocheted and embroidered and tatted. When she could find a free hour she joined us in the fields. She believed in children working as well, and could always find something for us to do. Except when we were doing our studying. She never weighed over one hundred and ten pounds.

My father was a "horse doctor"—a veterinarian without formal training. A farmer as well. He managed both by hiring a workhand to plow and lay-by, and with the family's help. Cotton was the main crop. Some corn and sugar cane and sorghum and soybeans. And there was Mama's garden. Papa would plow it and afterward she wouldn't let anybody else in it to work. A garden was her pleasure. She had a good one. A picture one. Some of that attitude rubbed off on me. Few people were ever able to suit me plumb in my own.

We children worked alongside our parents, hoeing and chopping and picking and pulling. Fodder is not thought much of now as stock feed, but back then we pulled every blade. Tied it in bundles and hung it on the stripped stalks. My sisters wouldn't work within sight of the road. And to keep from getting a suntan and freckles they rubbed their faces with cream and wore stockings on their arms and wide-brimmed hats on their heads. By the age of twelve I could pick a hundred pounds of cotton a day.

Before I was old enough to be enrolled in school, I'd sometimes go with my sisters. It was a two-mile walk and they often had to carry me part of the way, usually on the way back. I was small for my age. The only child who had to stand on a box to reach the blackboard. The teacher once asked me why I didn't come to school more often, and they tell me I replied, "I would wust Mama would let me."

I had a wonderful teacher in the first grade, a Miss Porterfield. The first day of school she wrote my name in chalk on my desk and handed me an ear of corn and told me to shell the kernels and make an outline of my name. We did this many times over and by the end of the day I had learned its shape and could write it on paper.

Those were stirring and changing times. We soon had a T-model Ford. A telephone. Screen doors. Subscriptions to the Georgia *Tri-Weekly Constitutiion, Farm and Fireside,* and the *Southern Cultivator.* The boll weevil arrived, and nutgrass. World War I was being fought. Schoolchildren gathered newsprint to take to school where it was rolled into tight bundles, dipped in hot paraffin, and sent to France as trench candles. My sister Inez won the fifty-yard dash on Field Day and the prize of a box of chocolate candy. After we had gobbled up the first layer, we found a second beneath and it was like discovering gold at Sutter's mill.

Aside from the Holy Bible, in our house were three books: *The Anatomy of the Horse; The Palaces of Sin, or the Devil in Society;* and a heavy volume with a missing back, *Cyclopedia of Universal Knowledge.*

The *Cyclopedia* opened my eyes to the world. Many a subject was covered such as you'll find in a modern reference work. And more still. How to prune a fruit tree. The language of flowers. Rules for games. The art of social correspondence. Good manners. Twenty-five sample words in several languages. A collection of classic poems. I got the poems by heart.

I wrote my first story when I was eight or nine. I still have it. I titled it "The Golden Nugget," and it was written with a lead pencil on a school tablet. Hard to read now, after seventy years. I found it recently and I'll declare that I saw my future in the piece. A foreshadowing, you might say, of all the scribbling to come. You might not catch it, but I did. It was not going to be the last. The itch to write was there. Along about that time my teacher was reading poems and stories to the class from the *Youth's Companion,* and I had read my first classic, Robert Louis Stevenson's *Treasure Island.* Both undoubtedly caused me to want to tell stories and write poems of my own.

I started a little magazine when I was ten. I had one subscriber—my sister Elloree, who was married and lived nearby. She had a box of folded stationery, and I used enough sheets to make an eight-page issue. I made up stories, which had to be pretty short, and I wrote poems for it. I wrote everything in it. I did a number of them, I don't remember how many. When I was eleven, I made a tent out of croker sacks and pitched it in the yard and wrote a poem in it. I still can recite it except for one line. It is stilted and formal. I used the word "dawn" instead of "morning." Yet, considering my age, it wasn't too bad a beginning. I was trying.

When I was in high school, I started a novel. It was about the sea. I had never seen the ocean, but that didn't stop me. I remember I wrote a while every night. I don't know what became of the manuscript. One summer I kept a notebook—a diary of sorts. It's not what is there that interests me now; it's what I *didn't* mention, what I failed to put in. It tells an awful lot about me. I left out all the things I think are important nowadays. I never mentioned my parents, and hardly my brothers and sisters. I seemed not to be doing anything that summer except picking blackberries and going in "washing," as we called it. Swimming. And I was regularly playing baseball—the things boys do.

And I'd got to see a few movies and I began to write plays. With croker sacks I made a curtain and hung it between two pillars under the house. The rear end of our house was high off the ground. We had moved to Shawmut by then. With the neighbor children as actors and audience I put on plays. One of my plays required a volcano, and I constructed the likes of one, one with smoke coming out. I don't know how we didn't burn the house down. And I was experimenting that summer. I made "gunpowder" to make firecrackers. I took charcoal, beat it to powder, soaked it in kerosene and dried it and packed it into a snuff box, and put a fuse in it. It didn't blow up but it popped. I was always into something. As now.

The boys I ran with claimed they wanted to be either cowboys or railroad engineers. I don't think I made a choice that early. It wouldn't have been either. None of them followed through. The ones I know about became weavers or mechanics in a cotton duck mill in the town, except one who became a textile superintendent. He had us all skinned in the schoolroom.

I became an author without expecting to be. I don't recall the slightest encouragement from childhood all they way through my school years. I didn't know about writing as a profession, something I'd be doing now and then all of my life. Nobody else in my family ever wrote or published anything. There was no precedent for me. I just wanted to write things down, to play with words. At first I had in mind writing a single poem. No thought of composing a second. Then, within a couple of weeks, another idea would pop into my head. The same with short stories. I'd compose one, and was satisfied for a while, and along would come another, and another.

All that was in Alabama. I had started high school in Shawmut and attended two years. Then we moved to Jarrett Station, a short distance from Fairfax, a textile factory town. I attended Fairfax High School and graduated in 1924. But I never got to read the great books until I attended Lincoln Memorial University, which was over the ridge from Cumberland Gap, Tennessee. I arrived with sixty dollars in my pocket, and I was starved for reading material. Every student earned his keep at LMU, and after morning classes I worked afternoons in the rock quarry feeding a rock crusher, and was the library janitor. When the library closed at night I swept the floors and emptied the wastebaskets and rubbed up the tables, and then with the door locked, the several thousand books and collection of magazines were mine until daylight. Many times I stayed the night, too drowsy to make it to the dormitory, and slept on newspapers in the storage room. I was like a child in a candy store. I hardly knew where to start. Somehow I found Thomas Hardy and Joseph Conrad and Hawthorne and Walt Whitman. The library was what Lincoln Memorial meant to me. I was saved by it.

At the library I happened on *The Atlantic*, about the most prestigious publication in those days. The library received gift subscriptions of several copies of each issue and after one was filed I had instructions to put the others in the furnace. What I did was save copies for myself. From donors would sometimes come issues for as many as ten years back. Or more. I kept scores of them and at the end of the term shipped them home. Those were the times of the Great Depression, and I had no employment, so I spent the summer reading. All of them. Every article, every poem, every word. I practically ate the paper. I learned from them

James Still as
a young man.

more than I can state. Even the art of composition, if it
can be said I ever attained it. I decided to write for *The
Atlantic*. First and foremost. The odds were great however.

I began sending verses to them (poems in their pages
were listed then as "verse"). I kept getting rejection slips,
but I didn't let them bother me. Mind you, I didn't submit
anything I thought unworthy of their standards. Eventually, I got a more personal rejection which read, "We at *The
Atlantic* have enjoyed reading your manuscript but regret
we cannot use it." And written in ink, "Try us again."
Finally, they accepted a poem called "Child of the Hills." My
first serious publication. Sort of started at the top, you
might say. A man wrote me several years ago to claim, "I'm

the person who picked your poem out of the slush pile at *The Atlantic* and insisted that Mr. Weeks, the editor, read it." Since then they have published three poems and ten short stories.

During those years Lincoln Memorial was having serious financial difficulties which accounted for our spartan diet. We students ate all the food off the table every meal. The university had an apple orchard and there were plenty of walnut trees on the ridges. We ate pecks of apples and cracked a lot of walnuts.

One year, what would have been my junior year, I didn't have train fare to go back to school, or the money to buy the clothes needed. That year I hunted work in several states over the South. The unemployed were everywhere. I walked. I thumbed on the highway. I sometimes rode the rails. One box car I crawled into was occupied by war veterans heading for D.C. to join the bonus army.

I rode out to Texas with some fellows and picked cotton for a while. We were in the fields at daylight and until dark. We baked in one hundred degree sun. My bed was a cotton sack on the floor. The drinking water was alkaline. It was too much. I hitchhiked and rode freights to Georgia. At College Park we rail-riders jumped off the moving train when news reached us railroad dicks were waiting ahead. In Atlanta, I tried Sears, Roebuck for a job. Other places, too. I signed up at an employment agency and nothing came of it. Up in Rome, I applied at a stove foundry. When I asked for work, the boss laughed. I was one of hundreds on the move believing there was a job somewhere. This sounds like hard luck but it wasn't for me in the long run. It was experience I couldn't have had otherwise, and seeing the country from a perspective I couldn't have imagined. I was able to get back in school in the fall when a professor heard of my plight and sent train fare and signed me up for a scholarship. All my university years, six of them, came through the generosity of others.

The class of 1929, my class at Lincoln Memorial, was unique. Some ferment was at work. Nearly a hundred books have been published by its members, which included Jesse Stuart, who was to publish many a book of fiction and poetry, and Don West who was to earn fame as a labor organizer and activist. I'll talk more about Don in a minute.

At Lincoln I was holding a work scholarship provided by a benefactor. As did most of the others. When I was to graduate I found out his name and address and invited him to the ceremony. Although he had assisted many a student, this was his first invitation. He actually drove down from New York in his chauffeured Cadillac. His name was Guy Loomis, heir to a sash and blind fortune, a gentleman in his eighties. At the ceremony I swiped up all the literary prizes except one I hadn't entered. One award was the Rush Strong gold medal for an essay on the value of truth. Afterwards Mr. Loomis offered to pay my way to a graduate school of my choice in the South. He also said, "I'll make it possible, not easy." That proved to be the case. I chose Vanderbilt University.

When I entered graduate school at Vanderbilt, Don West was there in the School of Religion. I hadn't known him well at LMU but in Nashville we became better acquainted. Both of us being farm boys, a city was a curiosity to us. On Sundays we'd go to town and wander about, and listen to the street-corner preachers. One claimed to be Jesus. A strike which lasted three years was going on at a coal mine at Wilder, up near the Kentucky border, and Don recruited me to go with him to distribute food and clothes and medicine that the students had got together. This was the strike where Barney Green was machine gunned to death. It was my first sight of people starving in America. In America!

When I graduated in June, my benefactor offered one more term of schooling, and in September I was off to the University of Illinois. A year later I was back home with three diplomas, no job, and no prospects. One of my professors, whom I had in some way displeased, had predicted that I would end up driving a team of mules hitched to a wagon. The prophesy began to seem not too farfetched.

I would have gone into the woods and cut trees for the CCC's—Civilian Conservation Corps—had they not turned down my application. I applied to the Library of Congress for a position in the reference department. I was catching at straws.

Then, I came to Knott County, Kentucky, to help Don West and his wife, Connie, with a vacation Bible school and a recreational program. Along with Don's son-in-law, Jack Adams, I organized three boy scout troops and three baseball teams. We camped and played ball all summer. Jack was to lose his life in the trenches in Spain in the late thirties. While in Knott County, I stayed a week at the Hindman Settlement School, and when I returned home they sent a letter offering a job as a volunteeer worker. They would shelter and feed me but couldn't pay me. I was willing, having no other prospects. The school was located at the county seat at the forks of Troublesome Creek. The hardtop road stopped dead in town, and a rutted wagon road took over. The bridge had washed out. You walked a plank, waded, or used a jumping pole. Or rode a high-water horse. I had come to the jumping-off place.

Hindman Settlement had no money to pay its staff. They could offer only room and board and laundry. Any shelter in a storm. The teachers were mostly women. Graduates of Wellesley, Vassar, Smith—mostly Wellesley. And a few men equally qualified. They taught during the day and tutored in the evening. Many had means of their own and had come for a limited stint. Say, two years. My assignment was the library. Yet with one hundred students confined to a fairly small campus it meant round-the-clock supervision by all hands.

The library was rich in good books and once a week— my own enterprise—I delivered a box of them on foot to some eight schools. I usually got to all every two weeks. A common cry from the schoolhouse door was, "Here comes the book boy."

I worked three years without pay. With the times improving, the fourth year I was awarded fifteen dollars a month. Slightly more the fifth year, and the sixth. For six years' labor I had earned an average of six cents a day. The publication of a few poems and short stories had kept me in razor blades and socks. And I'd published my first book, a collection of poems reviewers were uncommonly kind to. As I tell it, I was so rich I retired. On a day in June 1939, I moved to an old log house between Dead Mare Branch and Wolfpen Creek, facing Little Carr Creek. To reach it from the county seat you travelled eight miles over a rutted wagon road, and then more than a mile up a creekbed.

The log house I moved into was built in 1827, or as the state historical association claims, 1840. I went there to finish writing the novel, *River of Earth*, for which the Vi-king Press had offered a contract.

I had found a home. I don't have to depend on memory to describe that spring day in 1939, for I wrote it down: "A pair of black and white warblers teetered along the banks of Dead Mare Branch and minnows riffled the sum-mer pools. Partridges called in the water meadow before the house, and from the cove behind came an occasional *e-olee* of a woodthrush. A pair of rabbits flashed tails among the bluing weeds."

I knew why I had come there, but some of the neigh-bors were less sure. One said to me, "He's quit a good job and come over in here and sot down." And another who was asked who it was that had moved into the old Am-burgey place, said, "We don't know yet. We just call him the man in the bushes." I did sit down and finish the novel. Except for the wife of a widower who had been ordered through a Lonely Hearts Club from Arkansas, I was the first outsider to make my home thereabout. The thirty-one acre farm belonged to Jethro Amburgey who taught wood-working at the Hindman Settlement School. This house was his birthplace. He was the best known of the dulcimer makers and had learned the craft firsthand from Ed'ud Thomas. We used to think Ed'ud invented them.

When I first moved in I didn't know anybody. Getting acquainted didn't take long for I began to attend the community happenings. Depending on the season, bean stringings and corn shuckings and molasses making and hog killings. In the fall the pie suppers at the Wolfpen school and the school up Big Doubles. Both one-room schools. In June when sap was at its highest in the birch trees we went sapping. In time there were four of us who ran together. Sam and John M. Stamper and "Shorty" Smith were my cronies. Sundays we'd ramble the hills searching for ginseng, or pawpaws, or cane patches for fishing poles, or just looking. We visited old graveyards and half-forgotten homeseats, and I listened to their tales. The fourth Sundays in the month I attended the Old Regular Baptist meetings at Littcarr at the foot of the creek. The churchhouse, and Bern Smith's store which also housed the post office, was all there was to Littcarr. As I arrived in early summer, it was late to start a garden but I did anyhow, and as the frosts held off until mid-October, I had a garden full of sass—sweet corn, beans, squash, okra, cushaw, tomatoes, cucumbers and cabbage. There were plum trees and apple trees and walnut trees on the place. Come March I had my own cornstalks to burn when everybody else set fire to theirs the same evening and children danced about the flames. A rite of spring. At Bern Smith's store, and at Mal Gibson's a mile above me, I hung around a lot and helped the other loungers settle the affairs of the world.

Jethro Amburgey's five brothers were neighbors and I was soon acquainted. Melvin, the one living around the bend, came out the first day and asked, "Who's gong to do your washing?" and "Who's to do your cooking?" He said, "I want you to eat with us." I agreed to take supper with them five days a week. When I asked about the charge he said, "I just want you to talk to my children." Of course, I wouldn't go without paying, and I did pay. When the cow went dry we sometimes had homemade "beer seed beer," a non-alcoholic drink. When the dried apples came up short we ate vinegar pie.

In those Depression Days the people on Wolfpen and Little Carr lived almost without money. There was no welfare. No food stamps. Virtually no health services. Although whiskey would always bring in a few dollars, few resorted to moonshining. Honestly, to this day I don't know how many survived. They did grow big gardens and potato patches and a lot of corn, and they had pigs usually, and most had a cow. Not all. Still you need a little more, don't you? With children in school how did they keep shoes on their feet?

I also recall Jim Amburgey visiting. A distant relative of Jethro's. He sat in the door and hung his feet over the steps. I recollect he said, "I've been coming to this place since I was a child. I come here for a good drink of water. This is the best water well in the country."

Later, I got to know the coal camps, and I used to spend weekends once in a while at McRoberts. McRoberts was one of several coal towns practically linked together in the upper reaches of the Kentucky River. The Woodrow Amburgey family were among my best friends. Woodrow was a blacksmith at Consol, and a twin brother of Jethro's. I've never work in a mine, or expected to. Can't be at ease underground in so small a space. Yet I've visited them a lot of times. The last one I entered I thought I'd smother before I could get out. You can't pay a coal miner enough to fit the risk of death. And of black lung.

Actually, I don't see how the miners made it either. They lived out of the company store. The coal companies paid them mostly in scrip—their own money, so to speak. They printed little tokens with "Knott Coal Company" or some other operation on them. Pewter coins representing a dollar, or a fraction of one. And if someone wanted to draw money on their salary ahead of time, they'd loan it to them in scrip. They couldn't use the scrip except in the company store, and the prices were usually jacked up. They received little in cash. At the end of the two-week period they often owed the store all or nearly everything they had earned.

"You talk smart but you've got hillbilly wrote all over you."

There are a lot of natural born storytellers and I've encountered them here and there. In Wash Vance's store at Kay-Zee where he operated a grocery. Seated on lard cans and feed sacks at Bluestone in Rowan County. At Millstone, Mayking, and Mousie, and Hazard. In churchyards. On courthouse steps. Oral storytellers.

I can't name the exact year I started jotting down things they said in notebooks. I did it only for my own eyes. You might say they were written to inform stories and poems to come, yet I never thumbed through looking for an idea or a quotation. To write it fixed it in memory. The purpose of the notebooks was to cover every facet of life in my community as well as all of the county and the counties adjoining. Not just oral comment altogether. Not all the notes got into the notebooks. I keep coming across scraps of paper with notations which might have been included. I recall deciding the material in the earlier notebooks was too scrappy and in some cases I could hardly read my own

The Wolfpen notebooks: There are twenty-three of them, six by four inches, wire-hinged.

writing. I reworked the first couple and pitched out a lot. I used ink at first and later ballpoint pens or both, and I began to write in what used to be called library hand. Every letter clear. The period covered is roughly 1931 to 1965. The setting-down, I mean. What has been added since usually harks back to this span—the time we were living mostly in the nineteenth century, so to speak. Nobody else saw the notebooks until *Foxfire* asked to examine them. Before then I'd never considered publication. I did come to believe they might in future be of interest to folklorists and social historians.

After a time nothing was put into the notebooks directly. I'd write on a scrap of paper, whatever was handy, most often the backs of envelopes. I'd let them cool off a bit, a week or so, maybe a month, and then decide whether they were worth including. A tape recorder wouldn't have served my purpose even if I'd had one. I wanted only the meaningful, *telling* statement. I might extract a single sentence from a long conversation. In my limited experience with a tape recorder, I've found the speaker is often usually guarded in what is said. Confidentiality is lost. For my type of note-taking, this is important. As for a collection of oral statements such as I did record in writing, while many may not seem much in themselves, taken as a whole I believe they offer a picture of the region not otherwise provided. Another aspect.

I didn't own a camera either. Nobody in my community had one. What I did was to trace the hands of the old timers, about a dozen of them. Next to the photograph of a face, I think the hand speaks volumes. Form dictates function, it is said. These are the hands of men who used them as tools to make a living on the land and under it. In the fields and in the coal mines. Missing are tracings of women's hands. At that time it was not what you would ask a woman to allow you to do.

As I began nearly fifty years ago writing down what people were saying, we can know something of how they spoke and what they talked about. The most we'll know about many, for most are now dead, is what they said, and what I recorded. Anything anybody said, young or old, which seemed unique to the region. An example which comes to mind concerns a four-year-old child who died in front of my house one winter's night, along the creekbed road in the cab of a truck, of a burst appendix. She was being taken to a doctor. I had earlier written down statements by this child who had a quick imagination. She lives today only on a page or two in my notebooks.

Now and then I still hear remnants of the language spoken by Chaucer and the Elizabethans, such as "sass" for vegetables, "hit" for it, or "fit" for fight. People here are more likely to express themselves in an original manner than any place I know. I think it is something to celebrate.

Still wrote down on a grocery bag this excerpt of a conversation he heard.

I don't want or expect Appalachian speech to be like any other. It has its own individuality, its own syntax. To be unlettered is not necessarily to be unintelligent. It's a rare day when I'm out and about that I fail to hear something linguistically interesting. I go to the post office and I'll hear somebody say something that's of interest to me. That has a lot to do with why I live here. Of course, there are other reasons. I've traveled a bit yet I keep coming back like iron filings to a magnet. Here we are more conscious of the individual. Everybody is somebody.

Some of the people who come into the area expect to meet up with barefoot men packing hog-rifles and wearing black hats plugged with bullet holes. The "hillbilly" stereotype. Not too many lately as roads are beginning to open up the area and some are learning better. Naturally, if a visitor lingers a while he'll notice regional differences in speech and attitudes. Yet he'll find that human nature operates here pretty much as elsewhere. If you want to see what's left of the Appalachia I've written stories and poems about in the past, you'll have to leave the new roads and take up hollows and climb hills. Don't expect to find stereotyped characters in my fiction. Few fit the mold in reality.

But outsiders persist in believing that the woods are still full of barefoot men. Not so long ago the Settlement School was receiving occasional donations which reflect this view. Used Christmas cards, bundles of clippings from newspapers and magazines, and clothes of a type and condition the needy wouldn't be caught dead wearing. Once a truckload of books arrived and I had the job of sorting them. Only three of the hundreds were suitable for the library. We saved the boxes for the kindergarten children to play in. And I remember a man called me outside to look over discarded volumes he had brought as gifts piled in the backseat of an Oldsmobile. After he had seen the Settlement's collection, he climbed into his machine and drove off, taking his books with him. He had misjudged.

In those days the Settlement School had a hundred or so students. The staff taught by day and tutored in the evening. The first graduate went on to earn a doctor's degree at the Sorbonne in France, and others attended Har-

vard and like institutions. Two or three years ago, a man
came to the Settlement School from a college in Wisconsin,
and he said, "I'd hate to tell you what I expected when I
came down here. I've met more educated people and college
professors in this place than I have in my own state in
years." He happened to have come at a time when a resi-
dential conference was in session.

So, personally, I've never been bothered about being
called a "hillbilly" or "briar." They're synonomous—the
"samelike," as we say. I count it an honor except when used
as a slur. I was pleased when talking to a "gear-grinder" in
a restaurant in Jackson who thought I drove a coal truck.
After he had learned otherwise, and we had conversed a
spell, he said "You talk smart but you've got hillbilly wrote
all over you."

It's understandable local people have a distrust of anything written about the area. Even if the characters are
imaginary as mine are and the situations created. They
fear ridicule. Once in Joe King's store in Nickles Town a
customer came in and seeing me there caught his opportunity. He spoke up for my benefit, "Come a fellow in here
and he's writing about us. He don't know how we live." To
which I was quick to reply, "The hell he doesn't." I could
have told him what he had for breakfast. From whom he
had bought his likker. And something else I don't even
want to hint at.

People hearabout have long known I scribble, yet it's
easy to see it hasn't been profitable. Several years back I
was walking down the street in Hindman and met a prom-
inent citizen who greeted me, "Have you written any big
lies about us lately?" I stopped and said, "Yeah, Dock. I
wrote one yesterday. It was about you, and it only sounds
like a lie." It might be a comfort to some to learn that of the
eleven books published, every one cost me in time and tra-
vail more than I ever earned in royalties.

What my part of Appalachia had in common with other
parts for a long time was isolation from the main stream of
American life and neglect by both our state and national
governments. The neglect has only partly been addressed.
Yet things are changing. Almost from day to day. My nearest neighbor is spending the winter in Florida. There was a

time when the road to his door was the creek bed. Many saw service in the three wars of our day. They've had a glimpse of the world. Especially during World War II a lot of folk here about dug potatoes in Maine, threshed peas in Wisconsin, or picked tomatoes in Indiana. They went up to the factories in Detroit and Chicago and Cincinnati and remained. In recent years the downturn in the economy and homesickness have caused some to move back. Their children speak "buckeye."

Roads, telephones, shopping malls. This would appear to be all good. It's opened up the world and broken down barriers. Most families have a car or truck and move about on roads slick as a ribbon. Jasper Mullins told me a while back he failed to make a garden because he had bought a television set and didn't have time to tend one. There are losses. A sense of community is lost. Around me natural gas wells have done away with the fireplace which represents the cement which holds family and neighbor together. Between me and even the middle-aged there is mostly a "Howdy," or a "Hey-o." That's partly due to the generation gap. I'm considered an old-timer. There's only one other alive on my creek. We're survivors. Yesterday's people.

Actually, I don't think I was aware of the word "Appalachia" until a few years ago. I'm reminded of a stranger who stopped at a filling station near Hindman for gas, and who said to the attendant, "I'm from out of state. I'm down here looking around, looking for Appalachia. Where do you think Appalachia is?" The attendant answered, "Appalachia is over in Virginia. It's a town." And the stranger said, "No, no. I mean the area they call Appalachia." To this the attendant said, "I don't know myself, but if you'll go on down the road to the next station there's a fellow who'll tell you. He don't know either but he'll tell you *something.*"

I don't know where Appalachia begins, or where it ends. It's like a fellow once told me, "When I was in the eighth grade, my geography teacher kept mentioning Appalachia, and I couldn't find it in the textbook anywhere. I asked my Pap, "Pap, where is Appalachia?" And he said, "Son, you're sitting square in the middle of it." That's where I have a feeling I am and have been all these years.

"I would be a storyteller even if I couldn't write."

"I hope that by the second paragraph I've got you hooked."

I've never thought to write a story "about Appalachia." The background of my fiction to date is Appalachia, what I know best, and naturally my tales have a regional flavor. I've been asked, "After all these years, haven't you about run out of material?" I can't live long enough to handle all the stuff already in my head. Another question, "Are you still writing?" My answer is, "Am I still breathing?"

While I've had a number of adventures, both physical and mental, the greatest one has been the act of becoming a creative writer. It has been a way of life. Not a hobby. Not a sometimes thing. While I'm about all sorts of other activities, my center has been making words work for me. Many people come tell me they're interested in writing, but when I talk to them a bit, I learn they're thinking most of the *ends* of the business—publishing and possible income. Any writer of merit I know is constantly trying to find the time and a place to sit at his typewriter and indulge himself. It can be smothered down for a while, but if the urge is genuine, it will find some sort of out. It has broken up many a personal relationship. Don't expect anybody to understand. They won't. I've never found anybody who did.

Rather than thinking of myself as a *writer*, though, I think of myself more as a *storyteller*. I would be a storyteller even if I couldn't write. Anybody who stays around me long will hear a lot of them. Maybe more than he wants. There seems to be an endless supply. The old ones come back, new ones occur.

I've always written poems and have published a couple of books of poetry. But I ony write one when it overwhelms me. I don't sit down and say, "I am now going to write a poem." My poems happen in my head. A first line occurs, almost unbidden, and I'm on my way. Once written they seem to have preexisted. Like fishing for a loose pail and finally hooking it, and pulling it up.

Once I intended to write a personal letter I had put off for a long time. A reply was overdue. I sat down to type it, but, no. Of a sudden the first line of a poem popped into my head. "If the legs of the bird be broken . . . " It had apparently been in the making unbeknownst to me since I saw my nephew wound an egret in flight in Florida. I had chided him for unnecessary cruelty. However, the poem came to be titled "The Broken Ibis," for I had seen a picture in a newspaper of a wood ibis downed by weather in Kentucky. It was as tall as a man, and personified man. I empathized with the lost and bewildered bird. The empathy shaped itself into an idea which would not rest until it found expression.

This speaks of how one poem came into being. It doesn't necessarily apply to others. A recent verse of mine involved two events. The cleaning out of a water well, which is a dangerous undertaking, particularly an old well like my own. A boy did the job, for only he had shoulders narrow enough to squeeze through the top. His father managed the bucket. I stood by anxiously. He drowned at last at another time, in another year, in a flooded creek. "Apples in the Well" melded these events into one and I trust lent them significance.

After a poem is on paper I may play around with it, may change a word or two. Put in a comma, take one out. Punctuation is important. I call it "mental breathing." After all, you've got to get your breath as you read a poem, so you put a period. Give your reader a chance to collect his wits for the next sentence.

A poem needs to flow like a stream, distinguishing it from prose. You might say the banks control the direction. Emily Dickinson's "stairway of surprise" says it aright. It expands. Grows like a crystal in a chemical bath. It used to be thought music and the dance had some relationship with poetry. Modern poetry has clouded the kinship. It has lost much of its tonality. Explaining the footwork doesn't necessarily explain how poems actually get realized. The mystery of a poem is a part of the pleasure of bringing one into being. I never rationally expect to write another one, and then . . . and then . . .

You may write one in five minutes. Or ten. Perhaps fifteen. Allen Tate pranked with his "Ode" for a quarter of a century. Coleridge composed "Kubla Khan" in a dream, a dream disturbed. A recent anthology of verse is titled *The Made Thing*. Are poems made by hands? We do know that in the writing there are a host of things to do at once. All that you can know and are and can be comes together and is concentrated on a single point, like a glass drawing fire from the sun. For all the honor heaped upon its name, poetry comes a cropper on the market. Do you know anybody who has bought a book of current poetry this year? When Ezra Pound challenged a fellow poet to a duel, his adversary suggested that they stand at twenty paces and fire their unsold volumes of verse at each other.

In writing a novel there is more freedom. You are in charge. You can play God, be omnipotent. Be everywhere, or nowhere. You can know unspoken thoughts and motives. You can ramble up to a point. Stick out your elbows verbally. The writing of one goes on a long time. Every morning there's something to look forward to. A trip of discovery. You are many people, in succession. Words at work. That's the true reward. I never knew a writer whose efforts I respected who was not in love with the dictionary. They're not satisfied with just one. They're all over the place. My problem of looking up a word is that I may find myself at play there an hour later.

I might mention here that nearly all my stories and poems come out of something somebody said or I read in the newspaper—maybe an anecdote I heard that sticks in the mind like a burr and doesn't go away. First thing I know, a character invents himself and becomes a real person, and every once in a while, I'm thinking about him. Until my character starts talking to me, though, I'm not making progress. He'll speak his own words. He'll get my attention and the first thing I know, he'll be talking to me and I'll start making notes. My characters name themselves. Until that happens, I'll call him "John" or "Mary" until he or she tells me their name. There's a lot of name symbolism in my stories—Godey Spurlock, for example.

And I think a story should not only sound like truth but in a sense it has to come true. Also be logical. I hope that my readers will think it's honest. And it has to be psychologically sound as well. Take the story, "The Nest." I remember the act of writing it. A painful experience. I would never have thought about writing it except that at Hindman, a senior left school before he was to graduate to marry a young widow with a child—a daughter. They lived on lower Troublesome Creek in one of the hollows. The child was about five or six. The father and mother went on a visit for the weekend and sent her to stay with grandparents, just around the curve. She knew the way, had been there many times yet she became lost and spent two nights on the mountain in subzero weather. She somehow survived. I've been told that her cheeks froze and burst. She's alive today, though I've never met her.

Somehow she learned about the story, and she tells people it is hers. In a way it is. The happening bothered me. It stayed with me, preyed on me. By itself it wasn't a story. An incident. In the beginning it was no more than I've told you here. That's all I had to go on. Then eventually it evolved into "The Nest."

I don't usually remember much about writing a story, but I remember this one. It's written as a series of flashbacks. As the child climbed the mountain, I kept giving the reader a varied narrative. No repetition. In a short story, every sentence should build. It needs to go forward. It should, as quickly as possible, touch a nerve and start a response in the reader—have the reader identify with the character or characters, and then with every sentence there must be additional revelations. A story growing.

Actually I used words of one syllable as often as I could. Well, it wasn't possible altogether but you'll find it simply written, and dealing with a problem in child psychology.

When she comes up against the rock wall . . . I don't know how a reader would respond. I felt terrible myself. It was as if it were true. I got the child down to the fence on her way home, and I couldn't go on writing. It was torment. I don't think I ever lived a story like I did this one.

About three weeks later, I took the child to the end. When she got down to a bench of the mountain it began to snow, she was numb and cold. And do you remember the line, "The bench had the width of the world"? I remember wondering if it was too broad a statement, but I let it stand. At a book autographing in Hazard last year, the mayor's wife told me she wished I had never written the story, and I asked, "Why not?"

She said, "It bothers me. I still think about it."

I said, "That's the reason I wrote it. It was bothering me, and I got rid of it."

So generally I don't know that I'm going to write a story. Something will have been cooking in my mind, and I'll really want to get rid of it, so let's say I want to have the pleasure of writing it too. I have, on occasion, just dashed off the first paragraph, knowing it already. Then I write the last paragraph because I have to know where I'm heading. In fact, I know the end before I know anything else. It comes in a flash, usually. When I've written that, I know where I'm going and what's to come of it all; then I start back at the first paragraph and head toward the last. Yet nothing exactly happens the same way twice. I don't claim to have a method.

The place to begin a short story is as near the end as possible. My view of it. If I get stuck, which I often do, I go back to the last paragraph and tinker with it. I don't know how other people write, but it's a game—it's a playground—for me. I don't exactly work—I don't *think* I work—I gambol hard all the way through.

Many times when I'm having trouble with a paragraph, I set it on the page as if it were a poem and I can usually learn what the problem is—the glitch in the way.

The short story called *The Run for the Elbertas* took longer than any I ever wrote. I got stuck a number of times. It's longer than most magazines or periodicals choose to publish. I remember writing it. I knew *what* I wanted to do, but not *how*. When I bogged down I'd go to the last paragraph and fiddle with it a while. Pretty soon it's like stirring concrete. It sets and hardens. I could work almost anywhere in the story I wanted to, and did.

But generally, when I've created the first paragraph, it will stand. That's about how it's going to be. And somehow the characters lead me on. I want a story moving from the first sentence. No request to the reader to hold still while I indulge in description. And I hope that by the second paragraph, I've got you hooked. That's what a writer wishes for. A short story has to be very compressed. A writer has to do so much so quickly: introduce characters, set some sort of premise, all that sort of thing. But while I'm writing, I'm not consciously thinking about technique or verbs or adjectives. It's just as if I were telling a tale, and I'm not thinking about anything except enjoying telling it. That's all.

Later I go back and take care of the more technical details. I don't let my concern about them get in the way while I'm first writing the story. I take out certain words. Change them.

There are words I personally dislike and don't use. Dislike them in any context. There are words I would never think of using. I want to keep the language fresh, to enliven, and to communicate.

Using dialect is truly one of the great problems in writing folk literature. Once dialect is written down, it becomes something else. It's rendered by misspellings, isn't it? Even to the person who has just spoken, it would look puzzling. And yet, to be true to local speech it can't be overlooked altogether. And to have a chance of publication, you'd better be careful in employing it. You'll find some dialect in my fiction, enough to give the flavor of the region. What I hope to do is to evoke speech. I see no particular reason, as a simple example, in dropping the letter *g* from the word *going*. Even if spelled correctly it will sound in the reader's head as they are used to hearing it. In one of my early short stories I used a lot of apostrophes. When I sent it to Edward Weeks, editor of *The Atlantic*, he wrote back, "Dialect is out of fashion." That's not to say a character can't speak idiomatically. Two novels I can name offhand which handle dialect expertly are Mary Webb's *Precious Bane* and Kentucky's Elizabeth Madox Roberts's *The Time of Man*. While it doesn't happen in these works, dialect can break the concentration of the reader. It calls attention to the writing instead of the story. I don't want my hand to show. I don't want the reader to know I'm even there.

I've had pretty good luck. Manuscripts have been turned back to me, of course, but I kept sending them out. If an editor returns a manuscript, I don't feel upset about it. They're not buying turnips today. Maybe next year or some other time.

My first book was a collection of poems called *Hounds on the Mountain*. It was published in 1937 by Viking Press in a limited edition of 750 copies, and then reprinted. It stayed in print for years. Once I asked my editor if it was out of print, and he said, "Well, no. However, nowadays we are just selling it to the people who deserve it." Eventually it had another printing in a limited edition by another press, and now this book is a collector's item. Wish I had a few copies.

An editor at Viking Press had read some of my stories before then, and when I signed the contract for *Hounds on the Mountain*, I agreed to two other books. The first of those was *River of Earth*. Don't think I had any specific purpose for writing *River of Earth* except to tell the story. I didn't know I was beginning a novel. I wrote the first section and sent it to *The Atlantic*, and they accepted it and published it as an article. They didn't call it a short story. I didn't like that at the time, but, of course, the beginning section doesn't exactly fulfill the short story rules and regulations, even loosely. It became the first section of a novel.

When the editor at Viking asked if I was writing a novel, I said yes I am. He wanted to see some of it, and I sent the first section and the last of *River of Earth*. They sent a contract. Later, I asked him if he didn't feel a bit concerned sending a contract with so little of the book finished. "Well," he said, "we held our breath."

And then I asked him if there were changes he thought I ought to make, and he replied, "We trust your instincts." The only thing they did question in the galleys were certain spellings of words. They follow a certain style manual, so they changed words like "britches" to "breeches"—words like that.

River of Earth came out in 1940. It's been around a long time. There are a lot of good novels that somehow didn't survive. I can think of some which moved me, and I wonder why they are not still in print.

When you ask if *River of Earth* is based on true events, I can say what Mark Twain said about *Huckleberry Finn*. He said there was not an incident in *Huckleberry Finn* that he didn't known about happening to somebody or that had come to him from some reliable source. I'm pretty sure all the events in *River of Earth* happened somewhere and they came to my mind. In a sense, almost any novel is autobiographical. However, *River of Earth* is not an autobiography, I assure you, although my childhood informs this book.

"I read an average of three hours a day."

I think serious writing should be introduced in kindergarten. Children should have good books read to them early.

While I was school librarian at Hindman and all of the grades had a period to visit once a week, we had a children's room with small chairs and a good selection of juvenile works. I would tell stories to the first three grades, telling them rather than reading them, and holding up the book so they could see the pictures. I might read such a story as "The Three Little Pigs," and then have them act it out. I'd find it necessary to caution the child playing the wolf not to actually bite the pigs. For the other grades I was the readers' adviser, introducing them to books such as *Robinson Crusoe, Treasure Island, Little Women,* and *Tom Sawyer.*

Everything is new and wonderful to a child, and that is why I like to deal with children. I wanted them to gain a familiarity with the library even before they could read. I would try not to do too much pointing out but rather let them wander about. I have always listened to children and have them tell me their ideas and feelings. All too often in school a child is not encouraged to speak up. This was my experience. The attention span is very short for first and second graders and needs to be kept in mind. They shouldn't be expected to remain seated for hours at a time. At the library during story hour period I'd asked them to stand up, up on tiptoes, and pick the imaginary apples hanging overhead. Once a child, the son of a doctor, looked up and said, "I don't see no apples." Shouldn't I have guessed that he was going to be a lawyer?

When the grade school was moved to a new location and I no longer had a chance to work with them, I moved on to another job.

For some fifty years I have read an average of three hours a day. A professor of mine in Tennessee years ago told the class that if we expected to get anywhere and be anybody in particular in life, we would have to do the work of ten men. Well, I decided I would at least read more books than ten average men. Most of it in nonfiction. I would

"For some fifty years I have read an average of three hours a day."

read more novels if I could find works of interest. I roughly divide all fictional works into two. One is illustration, the other is art. There are great works in both categories but I'm looking for the ones, the all too rare ones, I personally call art. I'm just curious. I was born curious about the world. I want to know more and more. And anything I can learn informs my writings. Isn't thinking the act of processing information?

Since I can remember I've always had an interest in primitive people and I believe it began with the first book read to me before I could read myself. A simple book with drawings about the Eskimo, loaned by a teacher. There were dogsleds, Eskimo boys, ice houses. I brought it home time and time again, and my sisters would read it to me. I knew it by heart, but I still liked to hear it.

In the years following, my interest grew to include the Indians of America, sparked by Parkman's *The Oregon Trail,* and the aborigines of Australia and of Tierra del Fuego and Polynesia. Not until 1971 did I begin to concentrate on the Mayans of Central America and make a first trip to the Yucatan. Since then I have spent fourteen winters in part in various countries of the region—Mexico, Honduras, Belize, Guatemala, and El Salvador and Costa Rica. I've visited the major Mayan ruins, some several times over. Besides giving myself a chance to step back in time, I work at why the Mayans, the intellectuals of the Indian people, have virtually disappeared from the face of the earth.

People have asked, "Are you writing, or planning to, about all this?" No. I'm still a tourist, but an informed one as I've made it one of my studies and built up a collection of books on the subject.

It was Maurice Herzog's *Annapurna* which got me interested in mountain climbing, and that was reinforced by a visit in 1940 to the Grand Tetons in Wyoming. I yearned to climb the shining peaks beyond Jenny Lake. I never did. Anyhow, could I not climb the Matterhorn? It was not to be. At least I could read about the subject and vicariously experience the adventure. Thus my collection of books on mountaineering, particularly those dealing with Mount Everest. Mountain climbers, more frequently than most adventurers, reach the end of their tether. It's often life or death. What do they do then? What are their thoughts? How do they react to the challenge? Once, during World War II, I was a passenger on a flight from Cairo to Khartoum in the Anglo-Egyptian Sudan when our C-46 lost one engine and the other was sputtering, threatening to conk out. A possibility we'd go down in the Sahara. I recollect my response and have been buoyed up by it ever since. The pilot managed a crash landing. As a spin-off from Himalayan mountaineering, I took up reading about the primitive people of the Tibetan plateau. One thing leads to another. My reading and interests have always been eclectic.

I'm often asked what advice I have for aspiring writers. I prefer the perspiring writer. Those already at it, no matter the age. Those not waiting for the magic wand. It's not the green thumb which produces the fine sass patch, it's the dirty thumb. Hands in the dirt, scratching. Certainly a good liberal education would be a gain. Your teachers are all at hand—the best authors of the past and present. And a mundane item—learning to touch type, unless you can afford a secretary. Editors don't bother to read handwriting. What I'm saying is you get ready. In all aspects.

For a number of years my aim was to be published in magazines I respected. And when I visited a college library where there were a great many publications, I'd pick up a promising one and the first thing to pop into my head was "What can I do for this periodical?" Yet I didn't wander too far beyond the range of publications I admired enough to become a subscriber. You should have a firsthand familiarity with any publication you hope to appear in. Just the other day, a woman came up to me and said, "I've written some stories and I don't know where to send them." How would you *not* know? You wouldn't raise a hundred acres of cabbages without some knowledge of where you were going to market them.

Beyond that, if my answer to such questions don't fully cover the subject, it's because a working creative artist has his own cave. Who knows what goes on in there?

And having said that, I might move on to say I will talk all around the outer rim of the subject of creativity, yet won't attempt to explain the creative art. Even if I could, which is doubtful. It's my one remaining superstition. When I was a child, we were told that if we looked into a water well we might see ourselves in our coffins. Thus I dare not peer too closely into the well of creativity. The true how and why. It might desert me. The best I can offer is a personal observation. I write best when I've achieved a state of free association. How does it come about? I don't know. It happens now and again.

If you begin to publish, reporters will find the path to your door. No matter where. I was early described as a hermit. The label stuck. A recent article describes me as having lived for fifty years in a log cabin back in the hills with no plumbing. That hardly tells the story. Once a former

"I was early described as a hermit . . . [but] I've always viewed myself as running toward the world, not away from it."

classmate was dispatched by a school we'd attended to bring me back to "civilization." I had to explain that the past week had been spent in the Library of Congress in Washington researching for a historical novel. One I never wrote. And the month before I had spent in the woods of New Hampshire at the McDowell Colony. I didn't have time to be *saved*. To be recollected is that I've spent a good number of years in classrooms. How do you practice hermiting in a classroom? Most of the three years I spent in the U.S. Army I couldn't have thrown out my arms without hitting somebody. One wise reporter commented, "Being a hermit is a state of mind."

I've always viewed myself as running toward the world, not away from it. I need people. They're my stock in trade. And I want a few of them to need me. William Peden in *The American Short Story* reported that my life span was 1906–54. Could this be an error? As a neighbor once said, "Dead folks don't know they're dead." I think I'm still alive and kicking. Don't give me out.

SAYINGS

 In the Haystack

"When you tear into a haystack you never know what you'll discover. A 'possum, a covey of quail, a rattle-snake, maybe a gallon of moonshine stashed away. Or, not unheard of, a pair of sweethearts bedded down."

"God sent the very strongest people to live in these here mountains. Otherwise they couldn't of stood it."

"Things hain't going to be no better no more no how."

"There have been frightful struggles to live any kind of life in these mountains."   —*Willis Weatherford, Sr.*

"A poet is the nearest thing to God."

"You may watch it and note it for yourself. A left-handed man always thinks he's in the right all the time."

"Don't get mad; get level."

"How air ye doing? Air ye over your sick spell?"
"I hain't climbing no trees."

"The rheumatism has struck the finger next to the baby one on my right hand. I'm lucky it's not my trigger finger."

"Now, no. My name hain't on the 'waiting list' to see the doctor. Somebody told me that if your name was on the waiting list they'd never call you."

"What have you got on your mind today?"
    "I'm thinking about the sun-ball trying to rise tomorrow morning. I believe hit'll make it."

"Roses are loud-lookers."

"I used to sell hides to the J. D. Glasser Fur Company before the second German War. For a 'possum hide I got up to two dollars, and for a skunk, seven to eight depending on the stripe."

"Back when hogs ran loose, you hardly ever saw poison ivy. They ate it for a living. A mule will eat it too. Manton Young claimed poison ivy wouldn't hurt him and with my own eyes I saw him pull some leaves and chew them, to prove it. They must not of. I never heard any more about it."

"I want to know the whole story of the pilgrims. Abraham was the first pilgrim. And there were some United States pilgrims too."

"Time was people used their muscles to get ahead in the world. Nowadays they work their mouths."

"Oh, my little sweet-chopping garden hoe! I can't find it. I'm lost without it."

"Things happen faster'n they used to." —*David Adams*

"When first I subscribed to a newspaper I couldn't find nothing in it I wanted to read. And when first I had a telephone put in I couldn't think of anybody I wanted to talk to. I'd got away from things and people. Now I read every harry-cane of the paper, and I talk to folks if they call me."

"I can tell you a good'un on them twin sisters. One day when they were girls they were sent to the barn to feed the calves. They put down two pans of shorts, and two heifers were eating end to end, so they tied their tails together. The calves started pulling, and one pulled the other's tail slick off. They tied a rock to the tail and throwed it into the creek, and they promised each other they would never tell it till they both left home. The day the second sister married they told it. Their pap said, 'I don't care if it is a wedding day, I'm half a mind to cut me a switch and wear the livings out of both of you.' "

"I'll bet money."
  "I'll bet more."

"What do you know that hain't so?"

"Here's how to name the baby's fingers:
    Little man,
    Ring man,
    Long man,
    Lick pot,
    Thumbo."

"I'll tell you one on my brother. There was a fellow who had a big knot come on his head, and my brother told him, 'I know a person over in Floyd County who is a faith doctor, and I'll take you to him and he'll do something, and the knot will disappear.' The fellow declared he didn't believe in such stuff but he'd try it. So he did. The faith doctor done something to the knot and said, 'Now your troubles are over. Within a day or two it will come off.' Well, what happened was another knot come on his head. He had two knots instead of one."

"When the Big Collapse comes I'm heading for Florida. A man I know down there is ready for it. He's got a farm and raises everything he eats. He has a cellar and it's full. And he has weapons—rifles and guns and shells for protection to keep everybody else away. He's

ready, been ready for a long time, and I can go down
there and he'll let me in."

"Yeah, we had old times here more and longer than most
places, but they ended overnight."

"My old uncle said he'd tell my fortune, and he looked at
a crease in my right hand, and he said,
  'Your fortune's bad, could be worse;
  Wasn't for your rump, your belly would bust.' "

"Ay, that sweet young'un! Hit's spoiled so sweet salt
wouldn't save it."

"How far to Cody from the forks of Troublesome?"
  "Nine miles and a fool's head."

"Hey-o, prettier-than-I-am!"

"Your garden is getting away from you. If you don't hoe
it soon you'll have to buy a snake-rake."

"He's just a fun box. Claims he's got an order in to Sears
& Roebuck for hens' teeth, wheelbarrow seed, and 'possum trees."

"He's knife crazy. All he'll talk about is a Bokar or a Case
or a Russell barlow. He says if a knife is sharp when you
buy it, it's a good knife. If the factory can't sharpen it,
nobody can."

"I'm a native of right here."

"They hain't nothing to books. Some of them have the
biggest lies ever was. I read in one where Chinamen
were the first to make paper. Why, hornets were making
paper before God even thought about making Chinamen."

"Ninety-nine percent of fox hunting is getting away from
the house."

"I sold a fiddle once because it played by itself in the night. I thought it wasn't meant for me to own it."

—*Clay Collins*

"I want everybody to stop calling me 'Little Old Nasty Thing.' "   —*Judy Gibson (age 4)*

"The truth never walked his lips."

"My weapons have names. I call my new shotgun 'Death o' Many.' "

"Millard Haggins told me something the other day, and told me not to tell it, and I said I wouldn't, and I've let that out mighty few times."

"Old Horney Head will get you if you don't straighten up and quit your mischief. He's the Devil, if you don't already know it."

"The trouble with the schools nowadays is they got all them play-diddles in the yard. Young'uns can't think about their text books for wanting to get to the swings and ridey-horses."

"That's the best gun ever laid to my day."

"Every time you turn around there's something to fix about a car. But after a while you get used to it. It's like giving candy to the baby."

"You'd better throw a little air into them tires. They're about to go flat and hunker up."

"Us little fellows have to scrabble for what we get."

"If you see some pore little underly children, give to'em, do for'em."   —*Martha Burns*

"That bed was so hard had there been a dime under the mattress I could of told you whether it was heads or tails."

"How they got by with shooting squirrels out of season was they put rubber suck-bottle baby nipples on the gun barrels to act as a silencer."

"You're late. We've been looking our eyeballs out for you."

"He doesn't spare to mash the gas pedal of his truck. He makes the tires cry like a baby."

"Hello, Snakebrains."

"When Death comes a-visiting up in this hollow, he'll get the one he's looking for."

"Down in the flat country, what is there to see? Here in the mountains the world is held up for us to behold."

"All signs fail nowadays."

"Here lately they're starting Christmas before Thanksgiving. Yesterday I heard 'Jangle Balls' coming from a store in Vicco Town."

"These shoes I'm wearing were so tight when I first bought them I had to wear them a while before I could put them on."   —*Willie Stewart*

"How many books have you read this year?"
    "Nary a any."

"Women folk have been trying to come out of their skirts and finally they've made it. They're wearing breeches and peddle pushers. Some don't wear enough clothes to go to bed."

"What's the news?"
    "It hain't happened yet."

"He caught the brass T.B. playing the juice harp."

"Nowadays women walk around in people's faces with not enough clothes on to wad a shotgun. My mother and

my aunts wore as many as three underskirts. They
didn't aim to be skylighted."

"What I worry about is the next future."

"I paid Huck Francis a dime to see his picture show.
Huh. It wasn't nothing but shadows on the wall."
—Uncle George Childers

"Dr. Lott said I had the most reckless bowels of anybody
he ever knowed."

"I have the rheumatism. I'm down in my gitworks."

"How did I bend my truck fender? You actually want to
know? What happened was I met a drunk white oak
stump squarely in the middle of the road and it
wouldn't move over."

"I'm suffering with the crazy head. I've cut me a walking
stick so I won't be running into trees."

> Hogs Killed Here Let Me No

"I started itching in places and I went to the doctor and
he told me if I'd buy a cake of soap and jump in the
creek with it once in a while it would stop. Right. Right
as a rabbit's foot."

"It's funny about hair. As a man get older it starts shed-
ding off the top of his head and starts growing in his
ears and nose."

"I'm up there. Over eighty. The doctor told me, says,
'You'd better keep moving. If you set down long you'll
never get up.' "

> No Hunting
> Aloud

"Yeah, bless your soul, sure as Sunday morning, I'm scared to death of dying. We all dread that stinking death."   —*Frank Hicks*

"The truth is what raises the fur on the cat's back."

"Death is not a strange thing amongst the people."
                                        —*Preacher 'Tater Bill' Smith*

"I don't believe time will ever quit."

"This is a wicked, wicked world. Except in spots."

"I bought and built with my army bonus."

"A body can remember afar back, and then again he can forget afar back."   —*Bill Cornett*

"The end of time is coming, the way folks are acting. It won't be long. Yet nobody knows when that time is, not even the angels in heaven."   —*Luster Summers*

"Old Ed'ud Thomas had a little goatee, but the hairs were scattering."

"If some bold-ass stranger steps up to you and asks a question that's none of his gol-dern business, tell him something. But don't tell him the truth."

"We've had a mort of deaths amongst the old folks the past winter, and coming the next one there'll be more. They live in drafty houses, a lot of them, and they don't eat right. Old folks need to be kept warm and tended to."

"The only hanging there ever was in Letcher County happened in 1910, the time they executed Floyd Frazier. Dr. J. E. Crawford told me he was ten years old at the time and he remembered it well. To the hanging come folks from everywhere, on horseback, in buggies and carriages and wagons and on foot. They come from several counties around. A host of people gathered.

"Dr. Crawford said there was a man selling lemonade at the foot of the hill below the scaffold, and he had two washtubs full. At a nickel a glass. J. E. didn't have a nickel. He was standing there with his tongue as dry as powder when it got close to hanging time and the man told him if he'd keep an eye on his lemonade while he went to watch he could have all he could drink.

"Dr. Crawford said that was the most lemonade ever he drank in his whole life put together."

—Frank Majority

"He has read many a book and I'd bet that in his head many a thought has been thunk."

"Learn me to read."   *—Teresa Lynn Perry (age 4)*

"The largest yellow poplar tree ever cut in Letcher County was on Lewis Creek, on the Poor Fork of the Upper Cumberland River. Counting the rings, it was four hundred years old, and it made eleven thousand board feet of lumber. Quite a bush!"   *—Frank Majority*

"We have several war heroes in the area who risked their lives overseas and who were recognized and awarded medals. We've neglected them and several have taken to drink. What we ought to do is to dry them out and show some appreciation and grant them the honor here at home they deserve."   *—Harry Caudill*

"Hell is not a haystack."

 Heaven High and Hell Deep

"Come and see us some damn time. We'll treat you so many ways you'll never come back."

"My pap believed in boys learning to work. He'd have us hoeing corn until the lightning bugs started winking."

"I'll never forget the rocky creek bed I grew up alongside of. I had too many toenails knocked off in it to forget."

"The hill I was raised on was so steep you'd skin your nose climbing it."

"Hit might not be true but I've heered it. They tell how in olden times when Kentucky was Old Virginia they come in here a family who were so stuck up they wouldn't eat onions. They didn't build themselves a log house like everybody else. Aye, no. Not fancy enough. They went to a cliff and dug out some black rocks and they built themselves a black rock house, with a black rock chimney. And when it was built they set a big dinner and invited everybody, to show it off. And they built a fire in the black fireplace. Them black rocks turned out to be coal and you know what happened. Pride didn't pay off."

"Talk about good ground. The dirt in my sass patch is so rich the fence posts sprouted."

"Beware of a visitor carrying a budget. They might be coming to stay overnight—or they might stay seventeen years like Old Aunt Hattie Stevens done to us."

"I like the comers-and-goers. Gol-dern the comers-and-stayers."

"During my boy days we lived on a hillside so steep we had to rough-lock the chickens to allow them to scratch."

"They moved up to Detroit and lived a spell, and now they've moved back here where nothing's going on. All they can hear is a bird sing."

"Outside of coal mining, I figure you could call Lewis Cook's operation the first industry in Letcher County.

The one started and handed on to him by his father. At one spot he could grind your corn, saw and plane your lumber, forge a horseshoe and shoe your horse. Yet that wasn't what got his name up in the books. He was the one who cut the rope when they hung Floyd Frazier on Schoolhouse Hill in 1910."   —*Frank Majority*

"My daddy, when he died, I couldn't hardly give him up. We used to hunt together and fish together and work in the fields together. My brothers, they went to school and became doctors and teachers and made something of themselves. I didn't know what an education was. Now my brothers are shut up in schoolhouses and offices while I'm out in the sun where I want to be."
                    —*Okla Thornsberry*

"I lived up there in Cleveland for eighteen years after I left Troublesome Creek. I worked out my retirement and social security. I never did learn to like a city. Now I'm back home, where I can stretch out, where I can breathe."

"I don't know how old I am. My birth was wrote up in the family Bible but they messed up the figures."

"Summertime, we used to hoe corn barefooted. Sometimes a big toady-frog would jump on my foot and its belly would be cold as ice. Pap used to go squirrel hunting barefoot. He went one time too many without his shoes and a copperhead snake bit him. Being he was a strong man he overcome it."

"I've got all my children married, and I've got'em living in houses right close by. I have them close so I can throw a rock at'em if they do something I don't like."
                    —*Basil Evans*

"There were so many of us in our family our pap and mam just named us and turned us loose."

"I was born and raised in a log house. They wasn't no windows. On days when it was hard cold and we couldn't open the door we had to depend on crack light."

"I'm akin to everybody on my creek, and I don't want to be."

"Betty Troublesome used to be the meanest creek ever was. Any minute the bullets might fly. I wouldn't travel it unless I had a kettle over my head."

"In their home everything is old-fangled."

"I could have spent the winter with my son up in Indiana. If I'm going to freeze to death, I'll do it at home."
—*Willard Collins*

"Since my boys were away in the army they won't work for nothing anymore. No free labor, they say."
—*Melvin Amburgey*

"Before we had this road up Little Carr it was slavish to try to get anywhere."

"I've raised three children and they've all got good sense."

"Mine is the best corn crop ever a crow flew over."

"Grandpaw thinks rocks grow."

"This is my farm, every acre of it. I own it heaven high and hell deep."

"Those folks lived in a house a rabbit could have crawled through the cracks of. Winter time, they'd have big log fires and you'd have to set way back. And they never washed their faces, and they've never paid the doctor a dime."

"They're as poor as whippoorwills and live nasty as buzzards."

"Raised in Letcher County?"
    "I was jerked up there."

"I allus dreaded climbing a hill steeper than straight up."

"My pap always insisted on burning wood in the fireplace. He said coal stinks."

"They live in the head of the As-Far-As-You-Can-Get."

"Pap wouldn't hardly whip me even when I needed it, but when he did he settled all debts."

"I've done too much hard-growing-up and killing-dead time on Troublesome Creek to love it."

"As a child he was always hurting himself, knocking toenails off, cutting himself, bumping into something. The time he busted a dynamite cap with a hammer and blowed a finger off his mother knew something had to be done. She changed his name. He was Manus then, now he's Ivis."

"Everybody who lives above me on the creek hain't got no sense."

"We're long-way-round kinfolks. Not enough to do much bragging. But I like him, and I do."

"That town-raised jasper moved up in the head of the hollow and tried to farm. Naturally he starved out. He didn't even know what makes a pig's tail curl."

"His family couldn't keep him here in what he calls 'these sorry hills.' They said when he tuck his first step as a baby he headed for the door."

"Us boys didn't fool around with fish hooks when we wanted a big catch of fish. We poured black walnut hulls into a standing pool in the creek and waited until morning. Next day every fish in the hole would be belly up."

"When I was growing up and hanging out with my playfellows at least I always headed for the house in time for supper. My sons, they can't see dark."

"You've got to work back'ards with young'uns. Something you want them to do, tell'em not to do it. Watch how fast they hit for it."

"He lives so far up a narrow dark hollow he has to break daylight with a crowbar."

"They aimed to draft my son into the army and I didn't want them to, and he didn't want to go either and get himself killed down, and I went to the draft board and I says, 'There's plenty of boys who love to fight and wants in the war. I say, let them that wants to go, go. Let them that wants to stay, stay."

"How much did that son of yours weigh at birth?"
   "Eight pounds and a tomcat."

"Attending the Old Carr school was a whole heap easier than chopping crabgrass on a hillside in the summer sun. It kept a lot of us tadwhackers in school as long as we could stand it. There used to be a verse which said:
   'Ruther to school go
   Than to corn hoe.' "

"In the spring when my stock runs of out of corn and hay and fodder I used to cut down a young beech tree coming into leaf and let them eat the buds. That way I tided them over."

"Sonny buddy, I can tell you I've traveled far in my life. I've been in three states—Kentucky, Ohio, and Indiana."

"Their house burned down and they just saved the clothes on their backs. Caught the children barefooted. Well, I went to a rag sale and bought a sack full of clothes and then sent for the children. I said, 'Dig in there and find you something to wear.' They said, 'Huh. You're trying to put off old second-hand stuff on us.' They held the garments up and made all manner of light of them. But they took'em. To the last rag."

"For my grist mill I use hail-grit rocks from Big Black Mountain. They look like they have hail balls all the way through. The eye-of-the-rock is where the corn goes in. The farther the corn gets from the eye, the coarser the meal."

"He was just fourteen and he was a fool about his grand-maw. He was her pick. His grandmaw was old, old as the hills, and she wanted a Bible to read in. So he stole her one. Was that too wrongous? Not by my counts. Oh, it was sort of a sin, but not much of one."

"That man who's living single on Dead Mare Branch, they say he's got books stacked from the floor to the ceiling. My opinion, he owns many volumes of devilish writing."

"Why do you live on Dead Mare Branch? A hell of a place."   —William Still

"Dead Mare Branch is heaven on earth."—W. T. Stallard

"Wherever you live, glorify it."

"Air ye friendly?"
    "Shore."
    "Do I know ye?"
    "Knowed me since the day I was born."
    "Then come in and drag up a chair."

"I was down in my gears and they put me in a hospital up at McRoberts. The first thing they done was to examine me plumb up to the forks."

"Back yonder when everybody was honest you could leave a hoe in the field and go back the next day and expect to find it. That was back yonder, son. Away back yonder."

"Don't think that because you're young you'll live to be as old as me. I'm eighty-six. You might, then again you might'n. Neither one of us might not live to see the cows come home tonight. Recollect there are short graves as well as long ones in the Carr Fork Cememtery."

"Us fifth graders memorized the presidents of the United States and how they stack up."
    "Who was the twenty-sixth president?"
    "Three-door Roosevelt."
                               —Lausie Amburgey/Mal Gibson

"Do you remember the little Bosley girl in last year's first grade? Had long yellow hair, never smiled. Well, she died last summer. She started bleeding and nobody could stop it. There was no funeral and no casket. The just wrapped her in a quilt and buried her."   *—Edith Orick*

"Do your grown-up and gone-away children ever come back home to see you all any more?"
    "Not right lately. Hardly ever. Scarcely at all. Never do."

"For nigh on to fifty years I was ashamed of having Cherokee Indian blood in me. For the last fifteen I've been proud of it."   *—Joe Begley*

"During my lifetime, I don't want to travel no farther than I can go and come back in one day on a mule."

"I've listened a little to that stuff they call classical music but I don't like it. Take that man Moose Hart. I made better music when I was six years old beating on a washtub."

"He stays up in his hollow most of the time and comes out just to buy his tobacco. He raises everything he eats and here lately is putting him in a tobacco patch. Doubt he'll be coming out except to vote. He's stayed up in his hollow so long he walks crooked."

"Shore I put in a big crop of corn. I've got four acres as green as your eyes looking at me."

"Us boys used to chase minnows and crawdadders in the branch waters all summer. That was our fun. We'd get so sunburned our heads looked like gourds."

"We walked from Hazard to Hindman in a single day, twenty-five miles if you count all the high places and the crooks in the road. Them days, if you wanted to go somewhere and you had no horse, you went shank's-mare. We done it withouten a bite to eat. And I'll tell ye, when we did get to belly up to a table we laid our ears back."

"I shoved my brother Mark and he fell down and stuck a stick up his nose. Pap, he grabbed off his belt and swarped me, and he swarped me with the wrong end of it. Hit me with the buckle and knocked me into a corner and floored me. He didn't mean to. He grabbed me up and said, 'Baby, baby, why do you do such things and cause me to do this?' Pap always petted us after he'd whipped us."

"Bald Point is the oldest graveyard in the county. There are slaves buried up there alongside their masters. They say Indians were buried there in the early days. Once I was helping move a grave to where it ought to have been in the first place. We dug down and there was a skeleton buried standing straight up. Grandpaw—he was watching us—he said, 'Boys, dig no more. We're not grave robbers.' "   —*John M. Stamper*

"I was born in this log house and I'll never sell it; I might give it away."   —*Jethro Amburgey*

"You're the first man to live on Litt Carr Creek who wasn't born here. Not the first person, though. There was a woman come here. Amos Lovell, a widow man—he's dead now—he ordered him a woman from Arkansas. She come and he met her down at Sassafras depot in Perry County. She'd been on a train three days and hadn't had a chance to shave—one of those women who grow whiskers. He wanted to change his mind when he saw her but he was stuck. He married her and they made a good match. She fitted right in amongst us. When he died a couple of years later she went back to where she come from. The Ozark Mountains."

"After Dial's wife died his children put him out of his own house into an old shed behind it. And him a full ninety years old. They had him sleeping on an old trollop of a bed and forgot all about what he'd done raising them. His children banged him around like that."

"There hain't much going on in this hollow I don't know about. I make it my business."

"His stepson got killed in the Hitler war and him and his woman started drawing a big insurance-pension. After then he'd walk into the store and say to us loafers, 'I'm sorry for you fellows. I used to be a poor boy myself.' "

Troublesome Creek Nicknames

Creek Bird	Fiddle
Little Duck	Tug
Big Duck	Hog Pen
Little Birdie	Sprattle Bug
Chicken Leg	Drag Breeches
Pig	Black Strap
Piglet	Do'-Bell
Rat's Nest	Bogger
Man Hoss	Jailhouse
Pop Cod	Knucklehead

"My son, James, he's independent. He's six years old, in the first grade, and he doesn't get along with his teacher. Yesterday she told him to do something or other and he told her he didn't want to. Then she asked him what it was he did want to do. He told her he wanted to put sticks of dynamite in her ears, and light 'em."

—*Len Slone*

"Look at them little chunks of boys playing in the creek and having a wild time and not knowing what's ahead of them when they grow up. I used to be a boy that age. You don't believe me, do you? I don't hardly myself."

"When my corn is in the crib and my hay is in the barn loft I make friends with the earth. I swear not to hit another lick until spring."

"Several wars were going on during my young days. The killings have stopped now and there are many tales about how they got started in the first place. Yet if it was your grandpaw or an uncle or any of your folks who got killed back then it's hard to forget. Every time you come across somebody blood kin to the other side you feel for your pistol."

"My first two baby boys looked good. The third was the ugliest as ever I did see. When company came I hid him. But you know what? When he growed up he turned out to be the handsomest man ever hulled out."

"Hey, boy, where's your shirt? The temperature is down to freezing."
    "Maw-Maw is washing it."
    "Haven't you got another."
    "You think I've got a jillion?"

"My grandmaw is a gossip, and a trouble maker, and she keeps my folks all tore up. Still, I love the old hag."

"Nowadays people are running all over the place trying to trace their ancestors. They come here in my store asking me questions. Did I know the name of their grandpaw's first wife? Which side did their folks fight on during the Silver War? They call it searching for their roots. Me—I'm going to let my ancestors rest in peace."

"I want to live so far from other people that when I hear a rooster crow of a morning I know it's mine."

"Them were our happiest days, the bad depression days. We didn't lean on nobody. What we needed we raised, or built, or hunted in the hills. Me and mine wasn't touched."

"When they do fall out with each other, nobody can hate each other like kinfolks."

"He had a bunch of children and the youngest was always his 'possum baby.' "

"When you see a cork bush in a yard you may know the house has been there for many a year, or there was one there before it."

"We're some kin but I don't claim it. We had the same grandpaw two or three grandpaws ago. His farm joins mine and he allus has had it in his head he owns my land, too. Declares he has some sort of a patent-deed to prove it. The case has been on the court docket for years and still a-setting there. He ran my daddy off this place when I was a tad, and later he run my oldest brother off. I'm here now and he's trying to run me off. Hit won't work. I don't run. Yet I don't want trouble. So what I've done lately is to write a Bible verse on a piece of paper which says 'Remove not the ancient landmark which thy fathers have set.' And let the wind blow it over into his yard. For seven days in a row I've done that. And I've asked God to do something to him. I'm a-waiting. I'm a-waiting for it to happen."

Children of John and Barbara Mullins

Marcus Jay	I V A
Pealie May	Mary Run-Away
Bonnie Gay	Rachel Stay
Ollie Fay	Ruthena Kay
Newton Ray	Burley Bay

"I was born on Wolfpen Creek and I lived there until I was fourteen. My daddy named me 'Universal' when I was born. I hated that name. On my fourteenth birthday I took down the family Bible where our births were recorded and scratched out the 'versal' part. That was the year we moved to the state of Washington and I've never been back until now." —*Uni Hale*

"How come Hippo? Hippo Post Office? Well, I'll tell ye. When it was first established it was on Quicksand Creek in Knott County, mighty nigh the Floyd County line. Moved over to Floyd later. How it got called Hippo? They put the office in a goods store owned by an old fellow whose name I can't rake up. I'll call him John. John was to be the postmaster. The question was what to call it—the post office. Now, all the time back when a customer had come into the store and asked, 'How are ye, Uncle John?' he'd answer, 'I'm never sick, and I'm never well. I reckon you could say I'm hippoed.' That's how come Hippo."

"Some years back when I was the nurse at the Knott County Health Office I accompanied Dr. John Wes Duke in his visits to schools and assisted him in innoculating students against typhoid fever. I recall one school up in the head of a long hollow where he said everybody was akin to everybody else. When we had finished he spoke to them, 'Children, I have something to talk to you about. All of you look like a bunch of dried apples. Your stock is running out. Now here is my advice. When you grow up, and get into your head to go sparking, don't go up the creek, and don't go down the creek, go over the mountain." —*Sylvia Auxier*

"I was born here. My Pap and Mam was born and buried here, and their people before'em. We hain't moving nowhere else no matter what comes, wet or dry, good or bad, hell or heaven. We'll be here when the Big Morning comes."

Sparking Material

"Today is my twenty-fifth wedding anniversary. I tried to forget it but my woman wouldn't let me. You know women, they keep in head everything you're trying to forget. When she reminded me I said, 'Jane, it's been twenty-five years but it seems like a hundred.' She laughed, thinking I was bull-ragging her, and I sort of was. By now she never knows when to believe me. 'Well,' I says, 'being I've put up with you a quarter of a century and couldn't run you off I reckon I might as well keep you.' And you know what that crazy thing done? She cried."

"When I got married I was fifteen and my wife was thirteen. How come we got hitched so young was—one Sunday we were running across a pasture field and she fell down. I fell down, too. We didn't get up quick enough."

"When I was your age, young and full of ginger, I wanted to take a bite out of every pretty girl I saw."

"I wouldn't of married the sorry thing but he kept coming around. He was there in my face more'n the times he wasn't there. I didn't even like him. Well, there he was, and there I was, and finally we done it. We got married. He's all right, it turned out. I wouldn't give him up now."

"Here right lately my woman's got a notion she wants to sleep with her head on my arm. Hit's got me right sore in the shoulder. I told her, 'Old woman, if you don't want me to die of the rheumatism, you'd better lay your head on your pillow most of the time.' "

"When I was sixteen I thought I was in love and it made me sick. Sicker than a dog. My pap tuck me to the doctor, and come to find out it wasn't love. It was worms."

"I wish we could swap wives like we do horses. I've got one I'd like to give somebody a ding-busted good cheating with."

"I know postive yore woman rules you. Mine will have her way even if she has to burn the waters of the creek. The woman is the boss in this country."

"All my sweethearts have got married on me. I've run out of sparking material."

"I had a wife but when I got so old I couldn't cut the mustard she left me. And yours will do the same."

"Both of her two sisters, both of them younger than her, they found themselves a man and got married. She never could. As the saying goes, she had to dance in the hog trough."

"Now, they told her that the man she was marrying had already buried three wives which proved that he had a white liver. Women don't live long with white-livered husbands. She wasn't put off. She said, 'I'll outlive him being I'm a lot younger. I'll live to eat the goose that picks the grass off his grave.' But she didn't."

"So she actually found her a man and got married! Well, she won't have to lean against a tree to grind her corn from now on. She can get her young'uns in bed."

"I agree with fellows not marrying sometimes. But who'll rock you to sleep at night?"

"I'll tell you about wives. After a while they stop being sweethearts, and the husband just becomes one of the children."

"More men have been killed over an inch of land than ever was over a woman."

"I sweat a lot, and I ought to bathe myself more often than I do but my wife won't let me. Says when she sleeps with a man she wants to be able to smell him."

"He's slow to make up his mind about anything, no matter what. Why, back yonder when he got married and the preacher asked him did he take the woman for his lawful wedded wife, he said, 'I do, I reckon.' "

"So them two got married. Huh. All I can say is two fools met."

"Old woman, you can't afford to get rid of me. I'm an antique."

"The next time I marry I aim to marry a mule. Not half so contrary as a woman."

"She keeps her husband on leading strings."

"John M. went turkle hunting on Carr Creek yesterday. Today he took his girlfriend some turkle meat to cook. He wants her to eat a piece and learn how to crawl."

"The next woman I marry, I want one that won't wear out like a cake of soap."

"O, he's a grass widow. He's got a living ex-wife. If I married a widow-man, I'd want his other woman to be dead so you could drive a nail through her head and she wouldn't know it."

"I used to try to spark the schoolteachers. I had pretty white teeth then. I was a soldier boy and one of them said she fell for me before even she saw me. She'd heard talk of me. . . . Now, don't believe every word I say."
—*Ken Risner*

"My woman won't let me go barefoot at the house, but I do when I get her out of sight. I'm thickening up my feet for the winter."

"That girl, what a good-looker! Why, I could pick her up in my mouth like a kitten, and carry her off."

"In my time I've been a dear lover of the women."

"He's always trying to get into bed with some female. Says when he dies he aims to crawl in with Old Mother Earth."
—*Kenley Craft*

"When you left us it was like the world had a hole in it and all the life run out."

"How did you happen to get to marry that good-looking woman?"

"I married her during dog days while she was stone blind."

"You're sparking at the wrong house. She's too big in her parts for you. She'll wrap round you like a black-snake around a chicken."

"When you go to spark that girl you'd better take a doctor along. When you smell her powders you'll faint four times."

"Gosh dog! Is she going to marry that sorry fellow? She'll be taking her ducks to a poor market."

"There are two kinds of love: the 'ground-hog' case and the 'cholera case.' The ground-hog case you can get over. With the cholera case it's marry or die."

"There's a good-looking woman not a couple of miles from here who has sent for me three times, and I ain't gone yet."

"What are you waiting on?"

"I hain't waiting. She's doing the waiting. I'm not about to get married again. That worries my mind the least."

"I wouldn't of got married the second time myself if I'd had a way to get a hot meal three times a day, and somebody to scratch my back . . . and you know what."

"There's a difference between a woman's toe and a man's toe in bed. Let a woman's toe touch you and it's like a note in music."

"My grandma has outlived three husbands. She says she's going to marry a fourth and shoe the mare all the way around."

"She a looker. Fair as a blossom. She can put her shoes under my bed at any time she's ready."

"Before you start going with girls you ought to take the shuck test, to see can you pee hard enough to make a shuck rattle."

"I'll buy no insurance on me. Now, no. I don't want my woman to be having a big time on my dead money."

"He's too old to marry. He's got a dead bird in his breeches."

"You'd think him and her were fussing and fighting, to hear them carrying on. Now, no. They just live at the top of their voices."

"He was up in years. At first he aimed to marry a pullet, but the Church got on to him and he married a hen."

"The two worse things to have in a house is a quarreling woman and a smoking cookstove."

"What did you say when you heard your son had slipped off and married that girl and her some kin to him?"
"Hell shot a buck rabbit!"

"He got mad at his wife and he had to take his anger out on somebody or something. What he done was cut down all the apple trees around the house."

"When it comes to sparking, I divide all the boys in the world into two categories—the ones from Hazard in Perry County, and all the others. Let some girl be lucky enough to date a Hazard boy, the others are as good as dead."
—*Susan Walker*

"I raised eleven children, me and my woman did, and gave'em as much schooling as they'd take. Now they're grown and married off and I'm a widow-man and as free as a summer grasshopper."

"When Carlos Higgins married his second woman she had a line on how he had treated his first one. She said, 'I want one thing understood. When I make up a bed of a morning, hit's going to stay made up. Not to be wallowed till night time.' "

"That's his really wife, the one he's married to. He's got two or three others he don't talk about."

"My husband knows a whole heap better than to step out on me. He knows I might catch him asleep and pour hot lead in his ear."

"In my school days anybody who had a plum granny in his pocket would have the girls after him. A ripe plum granny smells so famous you want to eat it but you can't. Tastes like a rotten cucumber. Yet for perfume they beat bubbies a mile. I've swapped many a plum granny for a kiss."

"I'd bet you my wife it's going to happen just as I've said."
"I'll not bet. I might win."

"My sweetheart, when she blushes she changes colors like a lizard."

"What I'd do if my husband started stepping out on me is catch him asleep, sew him up in the sheet, and beat the wax out of him."

"I'm off to see the prettiest girl who ever wore shoe leather and if I don't come back write me at Blue Eyes, Kentucky."

"He's been married four times and now the last'un has left him. He's a good horsemaster but he never learnt how to crack the whip at home."

"She got married at fifteen, and she done it just to get away from home and all the diapering she had to do for her baby brothers and sisters. The marriage flopped. Within three weeks she was back wiping tails."

—James Perry, Jr.

"He buried his old wife on Sunday and on Monday he put himself on a new pair of long-johns and cut a walking stick and set off to look for the next one. Somebody asked him did he think he could find himself a dough-beater at his age and he said, 'Any good woman will do.' "

"You can always find yourself a wife if you're willing to take you equals."

"Before I marry again I'd have to check with my dead wife."

"She's as free with her favors as toll-corn pouring out of a hopper."

"The first girl I ever kissed, or tried to kiss, here's what happened. She didn't know how, and I didn't know how. We bumped teeth, and that's all that happened."

"I'll tell you a good'un on his woman. She won't let one pillow rest on top of another on the beds in her house. Too suggestive."

"If he marries that widow-woman, she'll have him eating shit on a splinter within a week."

"How are you?"
    "Sick."
    "What do you mean 'sick'?"
    "I've got the sugar. Can't eat sweet stuff. The doctor told me I couldn't even kiss my wife."
    "Why, don't let that stop you. I've seen her. You can't get enough sweetening there to hurt."

"When he sees a pretty girl his eyes change colors."

"I'm out here in Utah in the CCC's and I want to know why in the hell I'm not getting any mail. I've wrote a meal sack full of letters and nobody won't answer back. You tell them damn girls on Little Carr Creek I said to go to hell, and they can kiss my brown spot."   —*Letter*

"You ought to get a thirty-day guarantee on that widow woman before you marry her. Recollect the last one you hooked up to lasted three days."

"You could get married again if you got out and looked for a woman."

  "Hard to do if you've got nine children."

"A woman is a lot of trouble. But I like to hear one walking around in the house."

"She was a widow, and he a widow-man. She was so deaf she couldn't hear herself poot. Well, I worked it up for them to meet, for they both wanted to be married in a bad way. I brought them together and they didn't know how to start talking to each other. Finally he asked, 'What time is it?' And she said quick, 'Yes!' "
                                                           —*Mal Gibson*

"Men and women get along better nowadays. Or that's the way it is in my house. When the old woman gets to fussing too bad I turn up the radio and drown her out. There's some good in the infernal machine."

"Rosamond's Lonely Hearts Club over at Isom in Letcher County is the place to go if you want to order a wife. She'll fix you up with one for five dollars."

"I was married once before. For a short spell. Me and her didn't hit it off much because she wanted us to live with her folks, and I wasn't about to. I told her that if I'd wanted to live in that house I'd of run her father off and married her mother. We stuck it out though. Nine months. Then she up and died from childbirth.

  "My right-now wife, we've been married fifteen years. I know it's been fifteen years because that was the year we ordered furniture off of Sears and Roebuck and got it washed away in the 1927 tide. Who could forget that?

Well, s'r, my right-now woman, she never set eyes on my first wife. Yet, when we pass the graveyard where my first'un is buried—well, you know what she does? She spits! Now, you explain that to me and I'll tell you why the sun rises every Tuesday morning."

"I've never figured how women make out without hip pockets."

"I know a man who swapped his wife for a mule, and it was as good a deal as ever made. All three were satisfied—the man who got the mule, the man who got the woman, and the woman who agreed to it. No rue back. I can't speak for the mule."

"Here I was in my early 30s and not married, and still trying to be. What I think was the matter was every brother and sister of mine had a set of twins in their families. It runs in the generation. Women don't mind having a baby, but they don't want them coming two at a whack."

"It wouldn't do for me to be rich and not have to work or worry about getting mashed up in the mines. I'd spend my time running after women. They tell me they're for sale up in Cincinnati."

"Her heart is as big as a cow's. She'll do anything for the neighbor. Somebody sick? She's there. She divides with the needy. She's the kind of woman I was hoping for when I married, and missed out."

"He was fifteen and her thirteen when they married. In the courthouse they didn't ask for ages for they saw she would soon be going to straw. They lived with his Pap and Mam. Being married didn't stop him from playing all day in the hills with us boys. She played with her dolls until she had a live one."

"I've quit having anything to do with women—except my wife. Every time I've peeped around she's told it on me."

"His woman handles all his business dealings. She carries the money. Her bosom is the bank."

"If I was a young woman again I'd set my hooks for him, and I'd bait it right to catch him."

"Sometimes me and my sweetheart would get too busy doing what we were doing and let the fire go out. We call that 'scaring the fire up the chimney.' "

Rule for Corn-Shucking Contest
(Stillhouse Branch)
White ear: 0 points
Speckled ear: 5 points
Skewbald ear: 15 points
Red ear: Kiss the girl of your choice.
First to accumulate 100 points: Kiss the girl twice.

"My wife is reading *Robertson Crusoe* to me and the children, a couple of chapters a night. We're way over in the book now. Robertson hain't got to the house yet."

"I said, 'Ah, Bill, I don't want to get married.' And he said, 'We've got this far, and I don't aim to give it up.' Well, we went into a marriage parlor in Clintwood, and we were standing in front of a clerk, and we were getting married, and you know the place in the ceremony where you say, 'I do,' Well, I said, 'I don't,' and I walked out."

"I tried one hitch of matrimony and I think I'll try another."

"The most trouble women have with men is that when a man is needed he's out of pocket."

"Tell John you seed me. He raised my young'un after my wife died. She's been dead twenty-two years. I'm a funny man, funny in the mind. I believe there's just one woman for a man, and the one man for a woman. So I never married again."

"All you girls face about,
Here I come with my shirttail out."

"There are men here and there who act like cowbirds. They slip around and try to lay their eggs in another man's nest."

"Somebody was trying to take his number two woman away from him and he heard about it. He went crazy mad! He knocked out three window panes and got on the bed and jumped up and down."   —*Mal Gibson*

"One of the pleasures of my life is to bring together the men and women who are dying to marry. I mean the widow-women and the widow-men."   —*Mal Gibson*

"The last time he offered me his sister-in-law to marry I said, 'I'll have to examine her, look at her teeth, see does she stem her fodder.' Well, he hasn't mentioned her since."

"When love comes to a rolling boil and can't be stirred down, it's time to get married."

"When radios first come in I bought me one. A battery set. When I turned it on all it would do was growl. I tuck it back. I said I've already got a wife and dog growling at me."

"If you're jealous of your wife and can't stay on the look-out every minute, get you two mean yard dogs."

"When they strung a telephone line up Spring Branch I was about nineteen and not too good to pull a rusty. One Sunday I called up Wiley Acres—called Wiley because he was sick in love with a certain girl—and I said, 'Wiley, I thought you ought to know. That sweetheart of yours is on our porch right now sparking heavy with another fellow.' Wiley, he believed me and he said, 'Goodbye, vain world!' "   —*Mal Gibson*

"Don't try to understand a woman. You can't. Just give up and not waste your time. They're beyond under-standing. What women want, I don't know any man who knows. What they say don't mean a thing. Some men get misled thinking they know a woman's mind by what she talks. That's a fool's road."   —*Lee Thomas*

"His daddy left him a farm, pretty good land even if it was steepy. A good man. A hard-working man. He was in the fields when he was supposed to be. He tore the mountains out. Raised five hundred bushels of corn a year.
     "Now, he was a little-sized person. No more'n three-quarters as tall as his woman and no more'n half her weight. When she got mad, and she sometimes did, she'd slap him around like he was a young'un."

"That girl—I'll tell you—if I got her in my arms she'd think I was a turkle. I'd put a lip-lock on her and wouldn't let loose till it thundered."

"Are ye going to hold the minnow bucket all your life and let the other fellows catch the fish? You've seen what happens to them who court too slow. Get married and stop horsing around. Hit'll settle your nerves. Your schoolmates have already got diapers hanging on the line."

"I seed in the paper where a woman seventy-nine years old married a boy seventeen. One thing I'd like to know—well, they's several things I'm wondering about."

"I went to his house shortly before bedtime because I wanted to speak to him about his bull jumping the fence and getting into my corn, and there him and his woman set, her in her chair, him in another'n, and he had his big bare rusty feet in her lap and she was pet-ting them. I reckon that's what you call love."

"I never got around to marrying her but she was a pic-ture. Aye, man! Another fellow got ahead of me. I did spark her a little before then. She lived on Sporty Creek, up above the Big Doubles. I lived on Spring Branch, two hollows below. I'd go to see her Saturday evenings about the time they lit the lamps. We'd set in the parlor and smooch. She'd have her hair in braids, and I'd tie them together under my chin, and when everything was out of pocket I'd go to the house."

"If you dance, you damn shore are going to have to pay the fiddler. The fiddler is going to have his money. Think about that before you get up on your feet. Or getting into anything else. I'm talking about more than dancing."

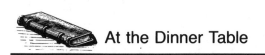 At the Dinner Table

"I love a good mess of parsnips. When I'm eating them I have to hold my hand over my mouth to keep from shouting."

"The woman who invented grease gravy ought to have a monument a mile high."

"What's for supper?"
   "Bread and with-it."

"When Russell dropped and broke the milk jar he lost his belly timber."   —*Jay Thornsberry*

"A lot of folks are living out of cans and pokes these days. And when they put it on the table it's not fitting to eat."

"The poor man's piece of the chicken is the neck."

"The way to make 'Low Gear Gravy' is with grease and flour and water. Let the flour brown then dump the water in, and stir."

"What I look forward to in the spring hain't garden sass. Hit's wild greens. They grow where God planted them. What you want to look for is plaintain, bird's-toe, fiddleheads, speckled dick and sour dick, mouse's ear, lamb's-quarter, hen pepper, blue root, creases, polk, shawnee, wild lettuce, wagon wheel, wooly breeches, and blue thistle. And don't spare the seasoning."

"Making hominy is a whole day's work. Recollect one gallon of corn swells to one-half bushel when it's soaked in hot water. That takes a day or two itself in the beginning. And throw in a tablespoonful of lye in doing it. After soaking, boil the corn for two hours in an iron pot, take off and wash. Boil it another hour or two, and wash it again. Keep your boiling up until the husks come off. A mess of hominy fried in hog grease is the best eating ever was."

"I've drunk too much sorghum juice and my bowels are as loose as an ashbank."

"During Depression Days the mines were closed and we lived on sour sop. That's buttermilk poured into hot grease and with cornbread crumbled in."

"At hog killing time what I like best to eat is the melt. I could eat it if I was tolerably sick. Some like the pig's chestnuts. Not me. Valentine Collins was crazy about the shoat's nose, roasted over a fire."

Buck Creek Stew
      Half a cup of water
      Cup of Moonshine
      Pinch of Ginger
      Dusting of black pepper
      Dab of butter
      Heat
      Drink burning hot.

"Her cooking! A dog wouldn't eat it. Her cornbread! You could knock a mule down with a hunk."

"There are seven kinds of meat in a turkle: pig, chicken, beef, turkey, goose, groundhog, and 'possum."

"They feed you good at their table. You'll never see the bottom of one of their dishes."

"Don't rush off here at dinner time. We'll cook the dishrag if we can't find nothing else."

"When I was a shirttail boy my Pap used to kill us a mess of snowbirds for supper in the winter time. A bite to a bird. Tasty as pig oysters."

Battery Bread
"It's a loose bread batter, cornmeal or flour, poured into a greased skillet and cooked on top of the stove over a slow fire. Turn often. Don't let it scorch. Comes to the table round as a groundstone."

Strawberry Honey
   One pint of strained honey
   One quart of wild strawberries
   Heat honey in sauce pan over slow fire, add berries, and stir until the two are melded together.
   Pour into jars.

Cincinnati Chicken
"Slice salt-cured pork belly. Soak overnight in warm water to remove salt. Fry unitl nearly done. Remove from heat. Cool. Dip in a thick batter of buttermilk and flour. Return to skillet and fry until golden brown."

Creamed Molasses
"Pour one-half cup of sorghum molasses mixed with one tablespoon of water into a skillet. Stir in teaspoonful of baking soda. Cook over low fire, stirring constantly until the mixture rises."

"We might invite you to dinner some time. We'll put the little pot inside the big pot and pitch in the dishrag."

"Wherever I go when I die I hope they have crackling bread for supper."

Kilt Lettuce
"Chop green onions, tops and all, into a bowl along with broken-up leaf lettuce. Add a couple or three pinches of salt. Dump into an iron skillet over a low fire and add bacon grease and stir like crazy till the lettuce is kilt. My mother, she always called it kilt. The best cure ever was for the spring fever." —*Hody Cody*

"When she boils coffee hit's so strong it will grow hair on your knees."

Fatty Bread
"After you've rendered your lard, grind up the meat skins and mix them in with your dough."

Hickory Cakes
"Boil half a cup of hickory nut kernels in a cup and a half of water until tender. Save the liquid. Mash kernels into a paste and mix with a cup of cornmeal, one-fourth cup of flour, a teaspoon of salt, a tablespoon of baking powder, two tablespoons of bacon drippings, and two eggs. Add the liquid and stir into a batter. Fry on a greased griddle."

 Critters

"Critters that walk the earth or fly the sky were put here the same as us and for a good reason."

"There's a serpent in this country we call the 'laughing snake.' If one ever bites you you'll laugh yourself to death. But I don't reckon one ever bit anybody."
                                                            —*Sam Stamper*

"Me and my woman found the first baby we had dead in bed. A cat had stole its breath."

"Ten ears of corn feeds one working mule a day. That's three thousand six hundred and fifty ears a year. There are a hundred ears to the bushel so you've got to raise thirty-six and a half bushels to feed a mule during a twelve month's time."

"We had that old cat and was she mean! She'd shore scratch you up did you mess with her. So troublesome to have around we killed her, skint her and made a banjo head out of her hide. And could that banjo *meaow!*"

"I've got nine children and seven dogs. I take care of all of them. I was offered a bunch of money for my dogs but they wasn't talking to me. Once a jasper mistreated a dog of mine and I stomach-shot him. Shot him in the belly. The doctor said he wouldn't live but I said he would, and he did."

"Lausie has everything about the place too petted up. The other day he tried to go squirrel hunting and when he started the cats followed. Six of them. At the upper end of the barn lot our three dogs took after him. And at the end of the pasture gate the heifer came running. Hardly had he got into the woods than he heard the mule making for him.

"He just come back to the house."

—*Monroe Amburgey*

"The mule I bought is a stump-chewer. Give him a chance he'd eat the barn door except for the hinges."

"That dog has teeth in his eyes."

"I won't work myself, so I don't want to buy a mule who won't do nothing either. Somebody has got to do something."

"If my dog doesn't like you he'll pour the teeth to you."

"He was in bed drunk, and a cat crawled in under the covers and had a gang of kittens. He thought he felt something funny and he runs his hand down to feel, and he hallooed to his woman, 'Hey, Liz, come quick. My belly has busted and my insides are running out.' "
                                             —*Kenley Craft*

"When I was teaching the Pattern Fork School I stayed at the only place there was to board, with a family who slept of a day and made moonshine of a night. How'd you like to sleep with two dogs under your bed? And try to eat with two hounds looking at you, begrudging every bite? And discover dog hairs in the gravy?"
                                      —*Don Carlos Amburgey*

"You boys are like hogs under an apple tree. You eat and you sleep and you never look up to see where it's coming from."   —*Perry Slone*

"A pretty cow don't mean nothing. The ugliest cow a-going can beat the fairest producing milk."

"Hawks can't drink water during dog days. You can see them flying around and hollering for it."

"I don't mind cooking for a pack of foxhounds if the man who owns them will work."

"How many cows do you own?"
    "I've got three old skins."

"We used to have a saying about fleas and bedbugs: 'If the *sharps* don't get you the *flats* will.' "

"If my dog hadn't stopped to scratch a flea he'd of caught that rabbit."

"Any man who would take his family dog off and throw it away because it got old, or caught the mange, ought to have his hind-end filled with buckshot from a 20-gauge shotgun, so he'll sink, and then be dumped into Buckhorn Lake."

"A catbird nested in that bam-gilly tree last summer and raised a gang of young'uns."

"Look at that pretty milk cow standing knee-deep in rich clover! Everything in her favor . . . Now, if you had to be one or the other, which would you choose, a cow or a horse?"

"I'd want to be a horse. I wouldn't want anybody pulling on my bag twice a day."

"The cat is coughing because she has a hair ball in her belly. If you licked your hind quarters every day you'd get one, too."

"Herndon had this old dog and I'd bet he was a jillion years old. Didn't have no teeth and he just laid by the door, and Hern fed him soft stuff. His legs had give out on him. You could call him a member of Herndon's family. He knowed everybody by smell and if he didn't recognize you he'd let out a snort. Along comes somebody he didn't know to the door one day and the dog growled. The stranger hauled off and gave the dog a kick. Hern, he came to the door and he says to the stranger, 'Sir, that dog lives here and you don't.' "

"We call it the 'corn planter' bird. When it hallos you'd better show up in the field."

"A weasel is quicker than eyes. You may believe you saw one but what it was was the blue smoke of where it had just been."

"Somebody's old dog kept hanging around my gate and I gave him a slice of pork with a pod of hot pepper wrapped up in it and he tuck off like Lindberg. The last time I saw him he was out of sight."

"When Wiley's old hound dog died he loved it too much to bury it. Him and that dog were hunting buddies. And where he went that dog went. He wrapped it in his best white shirt and put it under a cliff in a dry place."

"When my sheep dog died I sort of died too. The only true friend ever I had. Stayed with me hard times and good. I don't know where dogs head up when they pass on but wherever it is I want to go there when my time comes."

"Tomcats, man or beast, will be to ramble."

"Listen at that air peckerwood driving nails."

EGGS

Laid by Country Hens

"You won't beat this horse for a buy. You can't hook her up wrong. Hitch her left side or right side, ride her or plow her, she won't balk."

"These dog-peter gnats, do you get one in your eye, hit'll burn like a coal."

"The deer-lick birds come on strong toward the middle of June. As sweet as singing in church."

"July is all katydids and hoot-owls."

"Watch it! Here comes them hell-roaring gnats."

"I call that a 'dog-turd butterfly.' Watch one and see where it lights."

"Houseflies are good things for what they were created. They were sent in Bible times to plague Pharoah, and I wish he'd tuck' em with him when he died."

"Our old hound has a bad, bad habit. He barks at birds in his sleep and wakes us up."

"Frank Hays saw a young rattlesnake one time and he said, 'Let's not kill it. Maybe it'll grow up and bite somebody.' "

"Did you ever see a dead gray mule? No, and you never will. They just fade away like an old Indian. I've been living sixty-four years and I've never seen one. And don't know nobody who has. Maybe they live forever."

"In my young-sprout days, when the man of the house died his heir would go to the beegums and say, 'Your master, he's passed away. I'm you master now. Work for me.' If he didn't do that the bees would die. They called that 'telling the bees.' When I go somewhere I tell my bees where I'm going and when to expect me back, for if I don't they may not be there when I come home. A-liable to take off and swarm."

"The bluebirds—what's become of the bluebirds? They used to come sit on my clothesline. Everytime I saw one I was helped up."

"That cow, dag-blast her! She stepped on my foot, kicked me, caused me to spill a gallon of milk. She's got no business being a cow."   —*Madeline Hays*

"A mule is half horse. That's what makes them so contrary."

> "Fight dogs, you hain't no kin,
> If ye kill one another
> Hain't no sin."

"There's an old saying: 'Just because they's a gander around hain't no sign they's a goose nest.' "
                                        —*Marg Slone*

"If the cat brings in a live ground squirrel, or a young rabbit, or a mole into the house, don't try taking it away. If you do, the next thing they'll bring you is a snake. Happens every time."

"I've seen right lately a peacock spread its fan. I saw it but I don't believe it."

"The only reason I'm selling this cow is it's a force put. I need the money. She gives three gallons a day and has the softest tits ever I squeezed."

 ## Mountain Horse Sense

"Yellow poplar makes good coffin lumber."

"The balk between the corn rows should be the width of a mule's rump."

"Corn meal that's not dried out proper makes stubborn bread."

"Goose grease is the main-est thing for waterproofing shoes."

"Plant 'taters when the signs are in the feet."

"When I was a boy I used to have headaches. I don't know why. I'd crumple up black walnut leaves and fill my cap full. I was told that would do some good."

"The time to plant beans is on the hundredth day of the year."

"Jimson weed grows in rich dirt, the reason it loves barnyards. As bad as it stinks, it's good for something. The Man Above didn't put anything here on the earth for nothing. Hit's good for asthma. Lovel Thompson got kicked off the Short Dog bus for smoking it, though."

"As Hiram Gibson used to say, 'If you don't pick the goose, you won't have any feathers.' "

"O, that Queen of the Meadow! The best herb medicine for children. Cures a bunch of things."

"On the north side of the hills the white oaks grow the slowest. They make the best splints for baskets."

"To cure a ruptured child, split a sugar tree sapling and pass it between the breaks."   —*Melvin Amburgey*

"Bread dough turns sad if it's left to sit too long."

"I make my own chewing tobacco. I select me some cured leaves and spread honey on them. And then I prize open a beech log part way and stuff the tobacco in and let it cure a couple of months."

"Every July I lay-by my corn, chop out the crabgrass, goose grass, careless weed, and foxtail. Crabgrass is the worse. Whoever created it didn't know the mischief they were making."

"A dry June makes good crops, it's regular been said."

"When the ivy blooms, it's time to rob your bee-gums."

"I had a pear tree that quit on me. Barren two years straight. Astor Amburgey told me what to do, said, 'Make it mad. Kick it, drive nails into it, cuss it.' I did. Every since hit's come across."

"We call these hard maples either 'whiskey trees' or 'sugar trees,' depending on what you need them for. Sugar trees if you're up to boiling down the sap for sweetening. Whiskey trees to make charcoal to use at the 'still. Charcoal don't make all that smoke for the Law to spot you at your business."

"Grow dogticks in your garden and the moles will never plow it for you."

"Corn is not ready to grind into meal until it's as dry as an old maid's kiss."

"The way to catch a fly is to charm it. I can trap a fly in my hand. All it takes is know-how. I've never wasted a dime on fly-slappers."

"Blinky milk—that's sour milk. Turning milk creates eye-bubbles. When the bubbles start winking at you it's ready to churn."

"If you come on a time when you think you've got nothing to live for, it's the end of the line for you and you might as well be dead, what to do is take a good strong dose of castor oil, and hit the shucks, and stay there until you have to get up. Your bowels have locked up your brains. Within a day the sun will be shining."

"A tea made from the leaves of Creeping Charlie is good for teething babies."

"To doctor a sprained ankle, mix chamber lye and clay and make a poultice for it."   —"Old" Rube Morgan

"I'll tell you how to quit smoking. Roll you a horse hair in with the tobacco and make it. You'll shun cigarettes thereinafter."

"The male mulberry never bears. If a mulberry tree is crawling with berries it's a she."

"Wait until the snow flies before you rob wild bees."

"There was put here on this earth at the beginning of time all the herbs needed to cure every illness. Hit's up to us to tinker and experiment and learn what cures what."

"In the days I was a young sprout, we used Japanese oil for everything from the croup to toe-itch. I can't buy it now nowhere."

"Chew dogwood bark for heartburn."

"Here's an herb that's good for kidney trouble. If you have to get up in the night more than once, go to the woods and find you a few runners of it and brew them into a tea. We call it 'pee-in-the-bed.' "

"If you scrub your wooden floors with water from melted snow they'll turn black."

"For a cut foot, take handful of clean dirt from under the doorstep that's never been walked on, and pack the gash full. You'll be walking on it pretty soon."
                                             —*"Old" Rube Morgan*

"Milkweed juice will cure warts."

"Plant a worm tree if you want a quick shade. The worm critters that feed on the leaves make good fish bait. But when they bloom—hell-o, brother! The blossoms stink worse than a dead dog in the summer sun."

"Tears are the best cure for sorrow."

"Dry snow scattered over a dusty floor and quick swept out will beat any carpet sweeper ever you'll buy."

"If you want your canned beans to taste fresh from the sass patch, cook a geranium leaf in with'em."

"Sassafras tea in the spring will purify your winter blood. Hit's good for spring fever."

"I'm taking the groundhog hide around to grandpaw's for him to make some shoe strings. The skin cured soft because Pap rubbed the brains on the skin side."

"Bam-gilly trees are good for a host of things. The sap is good to cure sores and I hear the Indians used the bark to calk their canoe boats."

"There used to be—I've allus heard it—in this country a vessel they called a 'tonic cup.' Whittled out of the wood of a rowan tree. If you were sick and tuck you a drink of water out of it, you got cured. I just heared about it, never could get up with it when I needed it."

—Whitt Thornsberry

"The only way for a wife to keep from getting in a 'family way' is to sleep with her feet in a churn."   *—Ken Craft*

"A terrapin shell makes a hell-dinger of a soap dish. A natural dish. You can't drop and break it. Lasts eternal."

 **Weather**

"When raindrops gather like berries on the bushes you can bet your thumb there's more rain a-coming."

"The worst sort of weather 'cast has been coming over my Philco radio lately. I'm of a mind to buy me another brand."

"Hornets are building their nest-es low down in the bushes. A certain sign of early cold weather."

"The wind was so strong it'd knock a fellow down and beat him to death after it got him there. Well, mighty nigh it."

"If there's a dry wind on the sixth of June there'll be no blackberries for picking in July, and no beechnut mast for the hogs in the fall."

"When the crows keep cawing and won't hardly quit it's a sign of real hot weather."

"The last winter of the Big War, icicles hung from the cliffs like jaggers of glass."

"It was froze a time as ever you saw or felt. And I had to shank it eight miles with the weather bumping zero. My hands got so cold they cried."

"It made out to rain today, but when it come down to it, it didn't."

"Last February was the worst froze time ever was, except for one day. On Ground Hog Day the sun came out warm as wool."

"Any man can learn to read the weather if they'll watch it for fifty years. The wind clouds are the ones with the yellow spots in them."

"The moon is flat on its back. Look out for a change in the weather."

"Look at that moon fulling up! If it gets any bigger it's liable to bust."

"Everybody is sort of scared of her. She has the power to see-through, to know what's going to happen before it happens. She foretells weather too, and sometimes she hits it."

"Hit's them fellows walking on the moon that has messed up the weather."   —Wash Vance

"These atomic bombs they're letting off are ruining the weather. Hit's getting as bad as in the days of the Baptist Tower."

"Tomorrow is February 2, Groundhog Day. If the groundhog sees its shadow there'll be six weeks of sorry weather, and if it doesn't see its shadow there'll be six weeks of sorry weather. Groundhog don't know what I know."   —*Frank Majority*

"If it rains on the fourth of July, there'll be no grapes in the fall."

"This is redbud winter. Don't let anybody tell you it's dogwood winter. Dogwood winter is due when their blossoms are ready to drop."

"For every fog we have in August there'll come a snow this winter."

"The trees haven't yet put out leaves but they're studying about it."

"When there's a sort of mist over the sun and it hurts your eyes to look at it, old folks always called it a 'sun dog.' "

"There are several winters: blackberry, redbud, and dogwood. After they're past, sometimes we have Sick Bird winter. Birds get wet and chilled, look pretty droopy. Come a Jackfrost, they die in piles."   —*Martha Burns*

"We had a pretty good chunk of rain yesterday."

"When the old folks wanted a rain they'd look up at the sky and say, 'I wish hit would come a sizzly sod-soaker.' "

"Been raining pretty steady for a week. Now we need a good hard rain to settle the mud."

"Here it is February 15 and the water dogs are halloing 'spring.' They'll be looking through glass windows before it does come really."   —*Matt Combs*

"Did the flood on Troublesome Creek get into your house?"
   "No. It surrounded it, and washed my barn and coops and fences away. I hain't left a chicken to crow daylight."

"Old Lon Francis used to say the sun shines every Saturday in the year except one. He allus argued that."
—*John Francis*

"Back when we didn't have newspapers and no radios and nobody to tell us what the weather was going to do, we had Old Johnny Breeding, and you could ask him and he'd look up at the sky and tell you, and he'd hit it pretty good."

"When birds eat all the berries off of the poke stalks hit's going to be a rough winter."

"I come in home after that big shower wet as a well digger's rump."

"The rain went around to the north, then to the south. Then it come one of these middle-splitters."

"The hard rain we had the other day which done so much damage to the crops was one of the Devil's foot-washers."

"Pretty good rain last night on the corn. What you would call a 'nubbin-stretcher.' "

"When you hear a booby owl hallo it's going to turn cold."

"When the bee balm booms it's a hundred days till frost."

Rain Making
  "For a dust-settler: Hang one dead blacksnake by the tail to a sassafras bush.
  For a gully-washer: Two snakes.
  For a sizzly sod-soaker: Three snakes."

"Here's 'Hickory Shins' Amburgey's never-failed-yet weather prediction: 'If it doesn't rain, there'll be an awfully long dry spell.' "

 Superstitions

"My mother kept a silver dollar in a churn to keep the witches away. She believed that with all her heart."

"Sowing sage seed is sowing sorrow. Hit's bad luck. My neighbors won't plant it. They come at sausage-making time and borrow off of me. They want me to have all the trouble."

"A cow-lick on your head is a sign you've got grit."

"If you don't share your blossoms, your flowers won't grow; if you don't share your bread, your dough won't rise."

"If you ever find a plumb honest man, there'll be a patch of hair growing in the palm of his right hand."

"If you eat at the table with your hat on you're going to make a preacher."   —*John M. Stamper*

"A sniff of polecat is good for a bad cold."

"Carry a heart-leaf in your pocket if you want your pick of sweethearts."

"Never trust a baldhead man."

"Girls, if you want to be pretty when you reach sixteen, eat a lot of chicken gizzards."

"Ever notice your beard grows faster during a new moon?"

"To cure thrash in a baby, pour water into an old man's boot and spoon it into its mouth."

"Cussing rots teeth."

"The first three days of May are 'barn' days. No use to plant anything then, it won't make."

"When you shell your seed corn don't burn the cobs if you want it to come up in the spring. Throw the cobs in the creek."   —*"Mister" Jones*

"A dog bite won't heal so long as the dog is alive."

"Grandma told me the reason the back door of her house on Dead Mare Branch was painted blue was to keep the witches out. Witches only enter through the back door. They hate blue for a living."

"The ganders marry the gooses on Old Christmas night. That's twelve days after new Christmas. On Christmas Eve they're all mixed up again, ganders and gooses. By Christmas Day all have picked a mate. They're two by two. After they marry and raise their goslings they separate. The next Christmas they marry again."

"Anything born with their eyes open won't go mad even if a mad dog bites them. That goes for a horse, a mule, a sheep, and a chicken."

"Milk won't churn good butter while the elderberries are a-blooming."

"When I was a tad every house had a dream book. Did you dream a dream you could look up what it meant. Last night I dreamt I was dead. Maybe I've passed away and don't know it. Dead people don't know they're dead."

"Say a bunch of young people are setting around a fireplace and giggling, and say a cat walks in and sets before the fire. The first person the cat turns round and looks at will be the first to marry."

"Toady frogs are getting scarce. We once had one which lived under our porch. We feed it flies. It'd hop out once in a while and we'd pet him. It liked us. I figure you know it's the worst kind of bad luck to kill a toady-frog."

"On the first day of May put a snail on a slate and it will write your lover's name."

"Kill a frog and your water well will go dry. Anybody two inches between the ears knows that."

"Pick your geese on the dark of the moon."

"Bad luck to count how many turkeys in your flock. Count'em and a lot of them will die. I don't know why but that's how it adds up."

"When a baby smiles in its sleep an angel is talking to it."

"If a milk cow eats crabapples she'll go dry."

"Allus I've heard the human heart won't burn. The rest of the body can burn to ashes but not the heart."

"If you plow on Sunday you're liable to go to the moon when you die."

"Nail a horseshoe over the door with the points up if you want your next child to be a girl, points down if you want a boy."

"Anybody born while the mulberries are ripe has a good chance of being red-headed."

"When you see a cowlick sticking up on a boy's head, if he's not already into mischief, he's shortly going to be."

"You see for yourself I'm going to have a fine crop of corn this year."
    "Gosh dog! Don't say that. Hit's bad luck to brag on something that hasn't happened."

"I've put up with bad headaches off and on all summer. I

believe to my soul a bird got ahold of a string of my hair and wove it into her nest."

"If a girl knocks over a chair accidentally she won't get married that year."

"Sassafras bushes will take over a field. Cut them down and they come right back. Grub them on Ember Day and that's their end."

"The swamp violets growing along creek banks and in other wet places with stems a foot long we called 'hook-necks.' Us young folks, when we were sparking, we'd hook the heads of the violets, and pull. The one whose bloom broke off first would be the first to marry. If they broke at the same time, we'd marry each other."

—*John M. Stamper*

 Politics

"There's a condition I call a 'force put.' Something you have to do whether you want to or not. You can't beg off. Like being summonsed to set on a jury in a case you don't want to get messed up in. That's plime-blank what happened to me last fall. How was I going to get myself to do what I so strong hated to? What I done was I cut me a hickory switch, and I whipped myself to the court-house."

"There used to be the independent voter. Nowadays people vote in knots."

"He's hung himself on the thorns of the law."

"If you're so smart, why hain't your head in Congress?"

"Saylor is running for county court clerk in this district and the ticket he's running on is if elected he'll marry folks free." [Magistrates may no longer perform marriage ceremonies.]

"These candidates don't miss a chance. They even work a funeral like a bee in a rosy-briar, shaking hands with everybody."

"Kinfolks might cuss and fight one another yet mostly they web together when it comes to voting. If a candidate can swing over the one they look to, he doesn't have to waste time courting the others. Pay him and skip the rest."

"I promise you, be it I get elected jailer I won't get stuck up like the last one."

"Better not to have a case against him in the courthouse. He'll set there and blink his eyes and swear a black sheep is a white'un."

"I don't always vote for who I really want to. The good candidates don't offer me nothing. A man can't be blamed for voting bread on his table."

"I'm going to stop this sheriffing and start drawing my social security. Hit's a danger even for the Law to walk the earth. You're seen coming and they're ready to draw. I reckon I'm just a coward."

"Holding elective office is a lot of trouble. I wouldn't tackle it again. It was my kinfolks who made it rough. They all wanted on the payroll and some of them couldn't hardly read or write. As I'm akin to half the people in this county, you can understand the fix I was in."

"I wrote the President of the United States a meal sack full o'letters and he never answered a scratch."

"I wouldn't like him even if he was a horse."

"I tried to get elected constable the honest route the last time I run, and I couldn't. This time I aim to bust in. I'll get in office any way I can."

"Everything I own has a Democratic stamp on it. I wouldn't even buy a goat off of a Republican."

"The day I sell my vote will be when my cows come home."
     "You haven't got any cows. Not even a heifer."
     "That's what I mean."

"The first day the grand jury sets, there are these claimants with 'skinned noses.' They can't wait to indict somebody. Gee-o, they're mad! They are caving and huffing in the courthouse hall. If they're not called in the first day they cool off. The next day you can't see or hear tell of them."
                                                    —Matt Combs

"My daddy bought my first school job for me. Paid a trustee for it. The trustee told him 'I've already been offered thirty-five for it, give me fifty and it's yours.' The only way you could get a school then was to buy you one. They don't sell 'em now but you still have to vote right."
                                                    —Maxie Stamper

"That's the rule in this country. Anything you can beat the government out of, that's honest."

"I feel so sorry and no account today I wouldn't even vote for myself."

"So that sorry thing is running for constable. If he'd stick up one finger and count it he'd know how many votes he'll get. His own. He'll not stain paper."

"You mean there's no way I can persuade you to cast your vote for me?"
     "Wee hawkies, no! You can beat your gums all day and I'll not budge."

"They had me on the witness stand and I didn't like the pick-lock questions the lawyers asked. They got testimony out of me I didn't know myself."

"Come in here a fellow and nobody knowed who he was and he didn't tell nobody and he traveled around and he asked a lot of questions. That was when World War II had broke out. A paper fell out of his pocket one day and it got picked up and it was a map of the whole United States. That proved he was a German spy. Yet the Law let him skip free."

"I'd allow myself to be cut to pieces, salted, and hung up to cure before I'd sell my vote. That's an old saying that's been around a long time, and I'm saying it again and meaning it."

"What's that preacher doing on a platform with all them politicians?"
"He just said a prayer, what they call the invocation."
"He ought to do his praying in church, not amongst the crooks."
"Don't you figure them politicians need a little praying for?"
"I get you, I get you."

```
+-------------------------------+
|            Elect              |
|                               |
|        Amos Merryman          |
|                               |
|           JAILOR              |
|                               |
|      Chicken & Dumplings      |
|                               |
|         Every Sunday          |
+-------------------------------+
```

"Elect me jailor and if the sheriff locks you up for being drunk, the next morning I'll have you a little straightening-up toddy."

"He started off telling a falsehood in court, and then had to back it up with a pack more. He hung himself. I wouldn't be in his shoes for his socks."

"He has about as much chance of being elected county judge as a cat eating a grindstone."

"I'm going to take all the money I can get out of these candidates. Once they're in office they won't do nothing for me, or for anybody else. Just look out for theirselves. I'm getting all I'm going to get right now."

"The citizens of the county voted overwhelmingly against having a health department because it might raise their taxes a whet. We lost it in the ballot boxes but we won it at the counting table."   —*Craig Bailey*

"You didn't come along in time to know Fess Whitaker. Fess wrote a book about him being in the Cross Bar Hotel the election year he was a candidate for jailor. He got elected and let himself out. He was one of several Whitakers. As they used to say,
    Fred and Fess
    Little and Less
    Gid and Jim
    And all the rest."   —*Terry Cornett*

"Air ye going to the trial at the magistrate's court down to Vicco next Saturday?"
    "Who're they trying? What's the case?"
    "They're going to try and see can Big Bertha Hoskins sit down in a number four washtub."

"These politicians, what they say they'll do while running for office, they'll back up and do different when elected."

"Remember me? You don't? I'm 'One-Eyed' Zack Saylor who was in jail last year at Whitesburg and they had me working on the courthouse roof and I fell through and broke my foot. I was wrote up in the newspapers."

"When that coal severance money goes into the courthouse by the back door, there hain't much which trickles out the front. I believe that all the way down to my ankles."

"Over in Wheelright, back yonder, they had a mean sheriff who couldn't read or write. If he didn't know you, he'd walk up to you and whip out a stack of arrest warrants from his pocket and say, 'Look through these and see whether there's one with your name on it.' And you better not lie to him either."   —*Frank Majority*

 Moonshine

"I spent all the money I ever made on whiskey, except for the little I wasted on groceries."

"The time I pulled in the penitentiary for making moonshine was tough tiddy. If they ever put me in again it will be for singing too loud in church."

"He used to run off the best moonshine likker in the country. When you took a snort of his whiskey you'd better be standing on level ground."

"If you can drink the other fellow's likker, you've got yours left."

"There are three things you can't make nastier than they already are: tobacco, molasses, and moonshine whiskey."   —*Jonah Moore*

"Yep, he's stopped drinking, to hear him telling it. The fact is he's stopped drinking and started funneling."

"He's actually a quiet sort of man, but give him a few drinks and he's as loud as a jackass in a tin barn."

"He was so drunk he couldn't hit the ground with his hat."

"The way people are using likker nowadays is giving it a bad name."

"He's not much good. Can sort of get by, that's all. He makes a little likker and every bunch he runs off he scorches." —*Melvin Amburgey*

"Old man Thomas sold me a dulcimer once made of buckeye. He made'em out of walnut and linn, and any kind of wood, I reckon. The walnut ones costed the most. My buckeye dulcimer got broke and I gave it to Kinley Craft to fix. And he lost it, he said. My opinion, somebody offered him a pint o' likker for it, and that's how I lost it." —*Monroe Amburgey*

"John Bud got on a big'un. Once he starts drinking he can't stop. To get money to buy more whiskey he sold his mother's calf. It was so heavy he had trouble putting it into his pickup truck to haul it off. He fixed himself an excuse. He said, 'That heifer is too big for Maw to handle anyhow.' "

"You used to pass within twenty feet of my house up in the head of the Pud Breeding Branch, and me with two hundred gallons of moonshine in the house, and you didn't know it. . . . I used to drink a quart a day. . . . I'd work in the mines, then come in home and run off fifty gallons of mash before bedtime."

"Reach me one more little horn o' that likker. Hit's got a whang to it I like."

"In the whole of my life I've never heard a drunk say anything worth listening to." —*J. Alex Still*

"When I sight more'n the usual number of crocks of pickled beans in a warmhouse it's a never-failing sign the owner loves his dram. Regular drinkers crave sour stuff."

"During the Big Depression there wasn't no money. Couldn't get your hands on a nickel. You couldn't sell your corn or 'taters or hay. Couldn't sell anything except moonshine. You could always find a buyer for it and make a dollar or two. Some of us used to slip around and 'still likker and not let out we were doing it. That changed. It got common. Come a time we'd brag down at the post office how much we'd run off the night before."

"When you buy a pint of likker you're buying a club to beat your brains out."

"I keep just enough whiskey in the house to doctor sores, and to keep my throat from tickling."

"Old Son, just you sight that corn patch. I'd bet my thumb it would 'still up to a hundred gallons to the acre."

"It takes a whole pint of likker to prime him. That's when he starts in to really drinking."

"I used to be the worst drunkard ever was and I throwed it down. If I could, anybody can."

"I won't associate with a jasper who has less than a pint of likker on his hip."

"Don't offer me a dead soldier. I want one at least a quarter full."

"That spell of time I lived on Bill Dee Branch I used to make and sell moonshine likker. The good old yellow kind where the bubbles stay under when you shake it. I didn't sell it by the dibble-dabbles. Sold it by the keg.

Wholesale. Did come somebody just wanting a pint I give it to him. Christmas gift, whatever month it was."

"When I swore and be-damned if I'd ever swallow another drop of whiskey, the first fifteen dry days was a hoss."

"My three sons get drunk sometimes and they come in the house knocking over chairs and vomicking all over the place. But just let me take a little straightening-up drink, they don't like it. You'd think all they ever drunk themselves was sweet milk."

"Uncle Tolbert used to get drunk on Sunday, at a time when his corn couldn't look over the top of the weeds. Then he'd run into the barn door and hurt himself. That way he got us to hoe out his patch on Monday."

"I don't drink likker any more. It works on both digestion and my religion. I keep enough of it in the house to doctor sores."

"He's give up on me. He wouldn't sell me a drink of likker if I was snake bit."

"Dad-burn! Look at the price of a pound of coffee!"
    "When coffee gets more costy than likker, I'm drinking likker."

"I've never been sick a day in my life. Well, I mean I've never had anything the matter with me a couple of shots of Straight Creek couldn't cure."

"There have been two 'jenny barns' I've visited in my life. Gone now. Long gone. Anything that was a sin or against the law you could get there—beer, whiskey, yeah, anything. There was the Stiff Curve over in Knott County, run by an old man who wouldn't give up even if he was old. And there was The Snorting Pole on the Colson Road in Letcher County. Both stocked with good-looking women."

"I'm bone-dry now. Back when I was a drinker, I'd have to have a half-pint to see me through the night. If I didn't, I'd wake up jubious."

"This coming election I aim to vote for a sheriff who is not a drinker. I'd prefer one who has never tasted likker, or even smelt it."
    "If there ever was such a man in this county he's already been tuck. He's in the next world."

"He's called 'John Rub' because he practices drinking rubbing alcohol. They tell on him that early one morning he waked up with a hangover, and he opened one eye and peeped toward the window to see was it daylight, and there sat a screech owl with one eye open and one close, just like him. And John Rub said to the owl, 'I know just how you feel.' "   —*Ed Stamper*

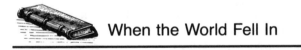 **When the World Fell In**

"He can load twenty-one shuttle buggies of coal in a day and every one with a graveyard hump."

"Before I'd mine coal for a living I'd make me a tin beak and go peck with the chickens."

"The water coming down Yellow Creek out of the mines will eat the fenders off your truck. It'll rot horses' hooves, too. What do you figure it will do to your belly?"

"I'm in for an unhappy summer. Them big coal trucks are running through my land and tearing my gate down everytime I fix it. I'm seventy years old and I've never killed anybody but that don't say I won't if I have to."

"I've got something to tell you, and you're not going to like it. Don't get your bowels into an uproar until you hear me out. Our boss at the mine fired us. The reason is the top fell in along the passage we worked yesterday. The cause the top collapsed, we didn't place enough props to support the roof. Let's be tickled we weren't there when the world fell in."

"I growed up rough as a cob. My pap put me through the flint mill when I was young. That's the reason I can dig coal all day on my knees standing in water and still go 'possum hunting that night."

"We're having labor troubles at the mine so I hate to see spring come and the trees get green and furnish cover. They'll be shooting at us through the leaves."

"He's worked so many all-days in the mines and so many all-nights at a gamble table he's older than he is."

"He's trying to double his power by working in the mines of a night and farming of a day. When does he sleep? And where does that switch-tail wife of his come into the picture?"

"Every day he took with him to the mines a quart of moonshine and along about ten o'clock you could hear his shovel begin to sing. He was one man nobody could out-load."   —*Clay Collins*

"Any miner worth his carbide can make a hundred dollars a day in good times. But them good times don't happen often enough. Not regular enough to buy bread and shoe leather the year round."

"He was killed in the same mine I worked in last week. I looked into his lunch box, and all that was there was potato peelings."

"I always carry a sun-ball in my pocket. Else how am I going to know in the bowels of a coal mine when it's quitting time?"

"I've dug all the coal I have the strength to dig today, and pay-day is two weeks off. I ought to go home but I'll have eight children looking at me and wanting something I can't give them."

"Monroe Lucus, he sent off to Montgomery Ward way back yonder and ordered a book on how to throw a voice. He learnt to do it, and he had a lot of big fun out of it. They say he was working in the coal mine once with a partner and the partner got mad about something and throwed his shovel down hard on the ground and the shovel spoke up and says, 'Hain't you ashamed treating me like a dog after I've helped you make bread for your family and raise your children?' That shook the partner up and he wasn't mad any more, and he picked up the shovel and says to it, 'You're the best friend I've got.' "

"The coal trucks have taken over the roads nowadays. When you cross it to the mailbox, if you don't want yourself ironed out, you'd better look both ways for Sunday."

"I've got the contract to furnish the Wolfpen School's fuel this winter. I've dug it out of the creekbed. Shore beats working in a coal bank on my knees manning a breast auger."

"I don't work any more. I mined coal for thirty years and ended up where I started. With nothing. What I live on now is a black lung pension check. But I've got to find a way to stop drinking."

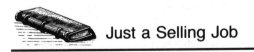 Just a Selling Job

"A good whittler can work on a match stem all day and still have enough left of it to pick his teeth with after supper."

"He's the boss. The man with the brass balls. When he speaks you're supposed to jump."

"Any schoolteacher who hain't never taught nobody nothing hain't never teached."

"They ought to be a story wrote about me, and what I done. Working for the Inland Gas Company I walked 160,000 miles in 24 years and 5 months. Crossed eight hills a day, every day, walking to check the pipe lines to see if there were any leaks. Hain't that worth writing about?"   —*Alka Hicks*

"He's the best teacher ever was. My children learned like rip under him."

"The teacher set him on fire. He had a box of matches in his pocket when she paddled him."

"The big hawk's done lit. I've been fired."

"Boys shun labor-work nowadays. They can't do nothing, drive a nail, harness a mule, or lay-off a piece of ground. And they don't want to learn."

"He's got more days work in him than brains."

"Last year on Snaggy Fork we didn't have a school. Just the name of it. Us scholars drawed pictures and played in the floor. The teacher set and read story books to herself."

"Don't hire him to work for you. He's shirky. He's slow as likker dribbling from the flakestand to the catch can."

"I don't want a first class mechanic job done on this car. Too costy. Do me just a selling job."

"If you don't ever work, and the government feeds you right well, you'll live a long time."

"He calls himself a schoolteacher! Huh! That sharp tack! He couldn't teach a fish to swim."

"He bore the name of being a good teacher but he wasn't. All he ever done was to tell us some animal story. We children nitnamed him 'Brer Rabbit.' "

"Ambrose Houndshell had a head on him so big he could hardly pack it around. Was a 'water head' as a baby, they say. He made his own hats out of bullrushes. A sort of a schoolteacher when he could get hired. Once he was over to the county seat trying to take an examination for a teacher's certificate and when he saw the questions he had the gumption to know he'd never make it. Yet he didn't hand in his paper unstained. He wrote a verse:

Arithmetic it makes you sick,
Grammar, I'm in low;
When it comes to geography,
Ambrose, you must go."

"I figured there was something going to come along and take care of me and my woman when we got too old to work, and here comes the old age pension. I'm saving of it what I can and when we die I want what's left buried with us. Don't tell nobody. There are folks who will dig you up for five dollars."   —*Uncle Bill Maxey*

Young man, show me your operator's license."
    "I hain't got none right now. I've got them ordered from Sears & Roebuck and they won't be in till Monday."

"That eighth grade teacher at Rock Fork School don't fool around when he paddles a scholar. He used one with a hole in it, to let the smoke out."

"Gosh dog! What happened to your face?"
    "I knocked myself in the head with a log-binder."
    "Always believed you were an expert at loading logs. You've been at it for years."

"For one minute in my life I was a damn fool. I got careless. I caused three teeth to be knocked out and one tooth drove into my jawbone."   —*Hill Hall*

"My schoolteacher is bowlegged as a goose and he has the kind of ears he can tuck a pencil behind."

"Used to be there were traveling tooth dentists. Mostly they pulled teeth. The one I recollect coming into our hollow could pull teeth like a chicken picking up corn."
        —*Orben Franklin*

"By doggies, you're sweating! Did you ever work hard enough to raise a sweat before? My opinion, a drop of that perspiration would cure consumption."
        —*John M. Stamper*

"I wouldn't hire Handley to hoe corn for me. He wears a number ten shoe and he steps on more stalks than he hoes."

"He lived to be ninety-nine. Claimed he was a hundred. Never worked a job in his life to anybody's knowance. Never planted a hill of corn, split a rail, or dug a lump of coal. Don't ask me why he didn't starve. He lived right here in my face and I can't figure it. Some said he lived by night, had him a 'still hid up in the hills, For all a body could see, all he ever did was set and grow whiskers."

"I don't need the job but I need the money."

"If you'll do a little work and get the sweat started the gnats will stop biting you."

"He stole my anvil and sold it for five dollars. What I can't figure out is how he carried a two-hundred-pound anvil off my hill in his arms and on a mile or so farther hunting somebody to buy it. Those were dollars well-earned."   —*Hiram "Shorty" Smith*

"The next trip you make to the foot of the creek drop in at the store and see what's hanging on the walls. Calendars. Dozens of them. The medicine salesman gave them to our tightwad storekeeper to be handed out free to anybody who bought a bottle of tonic. That skin flint! He never give nobody nothing in his life. It would tear out the bone. The hide would slip. This month the store has January all over the place."

"An education won't hurt you. That's what I tell my boys. Even if you turn out to be a ditch digger, you'll dig a better ditch."   —*Marlowe Speers*

"I told my Johnny Joe he couldn't make bread picking a banjo full time. He thinks he can. We'll see."

"What I'm waiting here in front of the schoolhouse for is if the teacher whips my boy again today he's going to get one himself."
    "Does he know you're here?"
    "He'd better do."   —*Puncheon Branch School*

"Ed'ud Thomas made his dulcimers on a turning lathe, turned by hand. Usually the face of the dulcimer was made of black walnut, the back and insides made of poplar. He had an old handsaw. Sawing a board to make a dulcimore he sawed it open flatways, holding it between his knees. He made that bureau we've got. My daddy paid him fifteen dollars."   —*Matt Combs*

"My sister, Tildie, could beat her husband to Boston chopping stove wood. She could stack up more in five minutes than him in ten."   —*Monroe Amburgey*

"Up in that there hollow, under a rock cliff where the sun can't find it, is the coolest place you'll discover on a hot day. When I worked with a road crew that's where we'd go after finishing a job on this side of the county. We had another spot nearly as good on the other side of the county. We'd finish a job and we wasn't about to go looking for another'n. We'd hide out till quitting time."

"So that's why we can't get the roads worked. My tax dollars have been going to pay you gents stretched out in the shade!"

"I've talked too much."

"When I hire a man to work timber for me I don't ask questions. His business is his business. Well, except, you need to know a thing or two. I don't want a man working for me whose boots are worth more than he is."

 ## The Nature of Man

"I don't start fights I can't finish standing up."

"He's about half fool but what sense he does have he uses."

"All them Halls are good musicians. Right from the time they shed their diapers."

"He was full fifty years old and so small he had to wear boy's clothes. But he allus carried with him the difference between him and regular-sized men—a razor-sharp Russell barlow knife."

"When I was a young, growing-up fellow and somebody would say something to me I didn't like, I didn't act mad. I'd just laugh. And the next thing I'd do was to up and knock hell out of him."

"If you're going to start hanging around my store you've got to learn to do two things: chew tobacco and tell lies."

—*Mal Gibson*

"She got so mad she like to of had a calf."

"I can take care of myself in a fight even if I am sixty-five. Not as good as I used to be, though. Up to five years ago I fit jaspers in their twenties and thirties, and won."

"You've known him all the days of your life and you don't want to admit it."
   "I've seen of him."

"If I have cause to pack a gun I want my 45-automatic. When I shoot a man down I want him to stay down. Not like when you shoot with a 22. Why, I know of a fellow who was shot eight times with a 22, and he lived."

"He wasn't born proper. Just sort of hatched out in the sun."

"The doctor has got my boy taking vitamins. All they're doing is stirring up the meanness in him."

"You figure you're too foxy to ever get caught up with. They's allus one other fellow somewhere slicker'n you."

"When my boys quit going to school I was so mad I thought at first I'd take a chair and crack their skulls. Later I decided it the best for us to heave and set and have a good time together."

"When my father sold anything, corn or oats or apples, he sold heaped-up-and-running-over. He'd give good measure, mete out justice."

"He's so sorry he ought to be stomped until the ground looks level."

"There are two Reecy Jones. The one who lives in the head of the creek we call 'Reecy-Up-There,' and the one living farther down, 'Reecy-Right-Here.' "

"He's got pretty good sense but he acts the fool so much you can't tell it."

"All he's good for is to set before the fire and to keep it chunked up."

"He's a grouch-ass. Always claiming somebody is trying to beat him out of something."

"Wicked? I'll say. The bowels of hell are yawning for 'em."

"He puts me in mind of a piss ant trying to swallow a bale of hay."

"Somebody is going to knock ten kinds of green apples out of you some day."

"If I can find out who shot out my windshield I'll take my knife and carve on him as long as there's anything left to carve on."
    "My opinion, some boy done it, with a 22-rifle."
    "Boy or man, I'll do'er."

"He can eyeball a tree and tell you within a foot or so how many board feet of lumber hit'll turn out."

"Young man, what you need is an old-fashioned straightening-up."
    "Do you think you can do it?"
    "Did I take a notion. But it's not my job, it's your pap's."
    "You're too beany-rumped to touch me. Try it and see who comes out winner."

"Stingy! He could live on a soup bone a week."

"He's so slow it wouldn't hurt him to fall out of a tree."

"Step back about two axe handles so I can take a swing at you."

"He lives in my part of the county, and I know him and he knows me, and yet he stole a dozen bushels of my pippin apples. I wonder if there will be apples in that place he's going to when he dies. If there are, they'll be baked."

"He's sorry—too sorry to throw a rock at a snake."

"I hain't no account. Tuck me a while to find it out. But I hain't lonesome. There's many another."

"He's the crookedest man who ever screwed britches on."

"After a person gets the habit of chewing tobacco I believe hit's a sin to punish the body trying to quit."

"Have you been knocked down today?"
     "No, and I'm not about to be."
     "Well, I might up and do it."
     "I might not like it, but you can try it and see. You never know how far a frog will jump until you punch it."

"All he knows is a chew tobacco."

"We called her Old Rag for her petticoat was allus hanging down."

"He sowed his wild oats as long as they would sprout."

"If I have to hit you I'll knock a home run."

"That reckless boy needs his leather busted every day."

"What are you up to?"
     "I'm setting here wondering where my next chew tobacco is coming from."

"You ought to of been to the box supper at Wolfpen Schoolhouse. Everybody got drunk, and they wasn't no Laws around, and we all had the best time ever was. Two boys tried to fight, and they didn't know how, and they just set back down."   —"Buzz" Gibson

"You'd better shave before somebody steps on you for a wooly worm."

"I don't want to fight or be fit."

"No man is better than any other hereabout. We all put on our breeches the same."

"This is Sunday, and as shore as Sunday comes he has to have a fight. If he can't find anybody else he'll jump on his woman."

"Did she fly off the hinges? She sizzled! Hot as a hen laying a goose egg."

"They give me a mean name but I'm not such a bad fellow. I just run with sorry folks."   —*Gar Maxey*

"He laughs at everything. He'd laugh at his mother's funeral. He's suffering with the cornbread consumption."

"When I get mad, the first thing I go for is my knife. So, if I don't carry one, I can't hurt anybody."

"You fellows didn't come back so I thought you'd got drunk."
    "You know better."
    "Not too much better. I had it in my head."

"He owed money to so many people he tuck paths through the woods to dodge 'em. He'd step on a stick and it'd break and fly up and tip his shoulder, and he'd say, 'I'll pay you tomorrow.' "

"The trouble with me is, everybody knows everything I do."

"Are you fellows about to fight?"
    "Now, no. We're just arguing to keep warm."

"Hud Thompson was gambling with Daud Hampton, and Daud was trying to cheat him, he thought. Hud said, 'If you wasn't so old I'd let you have my fist right between your eyes.' And Daud said, 'Don't let a few gray hairs make a coward out of ye.' "

"Fool with me and I'll do something to you the Devil never done."

"Sam Stamper was one of the best joke-tellers you'll ever hear. He can get off some real belly jerkers."

"I've got nothing for him. Don't call on me to help carry his coffin when he dies. I'd drop the box."

"Everybody ought to own and have to contend with a jackass for a spell. It would give them a good insight into human nature."   —*Proctor Wheatly*

"She had feet big as a horse and she tried to hide them. She wore shoes so tight she had to grease the heels to slip them on."

"Being born with a short waist, he looks too far down in his britches."

"Some men are so sorry they don't even pack a pocket-knife."

"Them Perkins boys, I went to school with them, and I liked 'em. But you had to fight 'em. And they were tough. You had to fight hard to come out on top."
     —*Vernon Hall*

"The people here not having been told what to do or say 'the right way,' do things their way."   —*Mary Rogers*

"There are people roundabout who'd think no more of killing you than they would to spit."

"Hain't no use picking up a tramp on the road. Take him a thousand miles and he's got another thousand to go. Yesterday I passed one who had thumbs stuck out both directions. He was traveling he didn't care where."

"He walks around like he's rich, with a big checkbook hanging out of his hippocket. All he's got is his ass and his elbows."

"Talk about slick! That jasper was as slick as owl grease. Could get by with anything the Law might try to stick him with. He could spit into a rusty lock and it would open."

"Recollect back when a pocketknife was good for something. Every man and boy had one. Couldn't go five minutes without using it to cut, carve, or skin. Meet a stranger and the first thing he'd say was, 'Let me see your knife.' As for whittling—you can get as big a habit of whittling as you can chewing tobacco. Whittling is good for the nerves."

"He wasn't thumbing me but I knowed him a little and I knowed where he was going, hunting for his next drink. So I picked him up in my truck. I'm not much for hauling passengers in my Big Mack on a coal trip. But I was running empty. I asked, 'Oscar, do you know me?' and he said, 'Shore I know you.' He didn't know me from Adam's off ox. And he said, 'I'd know them eyes anywhere.' Then I said 'Oscar, where are you going?' He said, 'I'm going to the moon.' "

"My mother never ironed my shirt-tails because she believed it would cause me to grow up lazy."
    "Didn't do no good, did it?"
    "Now, no."

"He's free with a dollar. He'll turn his pockets wrongside out for you. Everybody's got money as long as he's got some."

"If he'd treated me that carriony, I'd kick his rump until his nose bled."

"Back yonder on Spring Branch, if you saw somebody laying flat on a running horse on Saturday night and shooting every jump that was Hodge Bledsoe."

"Don't turn that greasy eye on me. I'm not guilty."

"Everything he touches turns to silver. He'll buy property nobody else would touch and pretty soon double his money back. Beats the hell out of me! I believe if he was heading for town and he picked up a rock and put it in his pocket, by the time he got there it would of turned to gold."   —*Richard Vicars*

"See that knot on his head? Somebody knocked him one. He deserved it and more. They ought to of given him another one to match it."

"Those rich folks who live in the big bottom in Hazard town in them fine houses, they think they smell better than we do."   —*Frank Majority*

"They baptised Old 'Bad Jack' Means last Sunday in the Kentucky River. Him who killed a lot of people in his lifetime. He claims to of just killed six. My opinion, his sins slew every fish in the river between Neon and Hazard."

"He's got nothing for nobody. Tight as a flush joint. His head is just a knot on the top of his backbone."

"Skinny! He has to jump up and down to make a shadow. His rump looks like two soup beans stuck onto a match stem."

"He was bad to fight. And he didn't win them all. Sometimes he got whipped. The other day he come into the store and his face was battered and he had two black eyes. I said, 'Knucklehead, what have you been up to? Sacking wildcats?' He said, 'Something like that.' "
                    —*Astor Amburgey*

"My husband can tell you where every fox hole is and every bee tree, and if he sees a dog he can tell you who owns it. But, let a fence be down, he'll never notice it."

"He killed Randall and Randall killed him back."

"He sets on the courthouse steps and whittles a stick as regular as geese go barefooted."

"A Harnett is hard to kill. You can shoot a lead mine at one of them and they're still coming at you. You have to hit 'em over the head with a sledge hammer."

"He's as slow as a schoolhouse clock."

"Enemies! They've hated each other's eyes since they were shirt-tail boys. Get these two together and hell is thrown open."

"She's so skinny you couldn't hear her trot through dry leaves."

"Goose-Hole Taylor—they called him that because when he was a tadwhacker his job was to stop the holes in the garden fence to keep the gooses out."

"Why don't you use your head for something else beside keeping your ears from overlapping?"

"My name is Hatfield. But I'm not one of them shooting Hatfields."

"He's so mean poison ivy won't break out on him."

"If I can't whip him, I can at least stand off and throw rocks."

"I made a big mistake but I've right-ified it with the man I done it to."

"What you got on your mind?"
    "I don't know. My mind is a-coming and a-going."
    "Better watch it. It's liable to go and not come back."

"My name is Tom Spurlock. I expect you know yours."

"Seems like my breeches don't hang to my hips right unless I'm wearing my guns."

"They nitnamed him 'Suckling John.' When the health doctor told his mother she ought to wean this eight-year-old son of hers, she said, 'What am I going to do when he starts throwing rocks at me?' "

"His really name was Smoot. From the smell of him he never tuck a bath. We called him 'Skunk.' "

"Has she got a mouth! Tells everything she knows, and a whole lot she doesn't. 'Big Mouth Minnie,' we call her."

"You may notice that folks with big ears live longer than most."

"If you keep your ears picked, and your mouth shut, and listen once in a while, you might hear something worth listening to."

"You'd think he was somebody the way he acts. Actually, he's shit on a stick."

"I'm a puore old tobacco worm. I've chewed it and dipped it and smoked it. I wish to God there was some other way to use it."

"He can saw a fiddle passing well yet he doesn't know what to do with his face while he's at it. He screws it up like a dying calf."

"Ross Turnbull is holding a shooting match up on Sporty Creek next Saturday. He just wants to see if he can get up with some of the guns rogues stole from him last summer."

"When he was a boy he ate gunpowder so he would grow up mean. It worked."

"She's so ugly she has to slip up on a dipper to get a drink of water."

"Nobody but a Caudill ought to marry an Adams. They're the only ones who can conquer them."

"He ate mutton so often you could smell him. We called him 'Sheep Meat.' "

"Your neighbors, when you sell them something, you don't charge them the full price."

"He wants to ramp and rave and cuss everybody all to pieces, and to do everything in five minutes."

"Every one of my children have a wild streak in them. I can't tell nothing about them, what they're going to do next."

"Let's get out our shotguns and have a splatter match."

"Me and him have got the same-like son-in-laws. Sorry. They're a shame to the Big Eyed Bird."

"A boy is plime-blank like a mule. If you don't give him something to do, he's into something."

"When he reaches for his can of Prince Albert tobacco to fill his pipe the dogs get gone. He follows throwing the burning match stems onto their backs. They's people that wicked in this world. The Devil is stoking his furnace for them."

"His name is Ulysses but we call him 'Useless.' He wouldn't work in a pussy factory."

"Some men my age use a walking stick. Now, I might come to it, but I hain't going to until it's a force put."

"Chewing tobacco is the old man's candy."

"Here's how much gumption he's got. After the war he bought himself a secondhanded jeep to conquer the rocks along the creekbed road to his house. There come a zero cold spell in February and the jeep wouldn't start. So he built a fire under it to thaw it out. Do I have to bother you with what happened?"

"He keeps several watch dogs in his yard but he's the one you need to look out for."

"This is how they tell it. I wouldn't swear hit's the truth. They say a *Courier-Journal* reporter was in Jenkins one day back yonder and someone had pointed out to him 'Bad John' Wright. He stepped up to John and he asks, 'Are you Bad John Wright?' Bad John says, 'That's what they call me.' And the reporter he says, 'Is it true that you've killed fourteen people during your lifetime?' 'Well, s'r' says Bad John, 'Right now I'm thinking about making it fifteen.' "

"My grandpaw was Claib Jones. He had the name of having killed eight to ten people in his day. I read that verse of yours in *Esquire* magazine with the pictures of our mountain people dancing around barefooted.* If my grandpaw were alive today he'd take care of you."

—(Letter)

"These old country stores, they're great places to set around and chew tobacco and whittle and play checkers and run down your neighbor's character."

"You say you've killed sixty-seven squirrels since the season opened and you're out to make it an even hundred?"

"That's the number I'm aiming at."

"If there was just one single wormy squirrel left in the whole wide world would you go for it?"

"I shore would."

"What makes us back in here the maddest is folks saying we all go barefooted and that we live nasty. I never left off my shoes except when I wanted to, and I bathe myself every once in a little while."

"Everybody has a little ornariness in them just ready to bust out."

*"Dance on Pushback Mountain," *Esquire*, October 1936. Illustrated by Eric Ludgren.

"Don't get feisty around me. I'll slap the taste out of your mouth."

"How much is that check you want cashed?"
"One hundred and ten dollars."
"We don't have that kind of money here."
"The hell you don't."
"We don't. We need all the change we've got for the business, and the bank is closed."
"You son-of-a-dog, telling me that! You've got it."
"No, we haven't."
"If I had my pistol with me I'd sink a bullet square between your eyes."
"Why don't you go get it. I'm always ready for jaspers like you."

"Three weeks ago I got shot. Fifty-eight buckshots in my legs. The doctor picked out some of them but couldn't get 'em all. They's one in my foot which bothers me most when I walk. I was shot for nothing. Just passing a man's house and he decided he'd kill somebody."
"In the past six years I've been shot twice. The first time was different."

"You can learn a lot about a man by looking at the seat of his breeches. If they're shiny, been worn slick, that tells the story."

"Look at him now, a big man. When he was born they could of put a teacup over his head. His mam kept his dress tail pinned to a pillow so he wouldn't get lost."

"I don't mind April Fool's Day. That's a lot of big fun fooling people. You can tell lies on that day of the year and see how far you can go with them. But Corn Night, now, no. Too much chicanery goes on and sometimes people get hurt. A rusty is one thing and chicanery is another."

"He thinks he knows everything. A regular sharp tack. Sharp as horse claws."

"Why do you kill birds you can't eat and don't even bother to pick up off the ground."
    "I like to see the feathers fly."

"I'll tell you why we have more than one ruptured man hereabouts. There used to be a big rock down at Aunt Sis Burgey's place which looked plime-blank like a part of a person. We called it 'The Kidney Stone.' Weighed up to three hundred pounds, say. I don't know how much. Maybe more. Well, sir, it was for many a year the thing to do for a young man to show his strength by lifting it, or trying to. One time or another we all tried. Two or three made it. I didn't. My guts would be hanging out today if I didn't wear a truss."

"There was this jasper who owed me money and I couldn't get up with him. One Saturday word got to me he'd just checked into The Rainbow. The Rainbow was a bunch of one-room cabins we'd nowadays call a motel. What I done was knock on the door of the one he was in, and he cracked it open, and I asked, 'What are you doing in there?' And I peeped in and saw this woman on the bed, and her ugly as sin. I know his wife and it wasn't her. He said 'What does it look like I'm doing?' And I said, 'If you want my opinion, you're not doing very much.' "

 Rooted and Grounded in the Word

"If the good Lord doesn't reconcile with you, you'll split hell wide open."

"They've padded the seats in their church, and that won't do. You know what the Good Book says about being at ease in Zion."

"When I get to heaven I'm going to hear the music of the harpers harping on their harps."

"He was a big preacher for our part of the country. Lived right himself and wanted everybody else to. But he wasn't against a man taking a drink of whiskey at the right place and right occasion. He'd say, 'It hain't the likker that's bad, hit's what's in the man.' "

"They's good preachers, and they's bad. I'd ruther hear old Linz' Mosley get up and grunt one time than to hear some preach an hour."

"I haven't been too bad a fellow. It will be an injustice thing if I don't get to heaven."

"When I die I want a wooden box. Not one of these fancy store-bought coffins. And don't put a white shirt on me, never wore one in my life. And bury me in a pair of over-alls. That's what I'm used to."   —*Hansford Austin*

"I doubt the Devil will let him into hell when he dies. My opinion, he'll have to stay at the half-way place."

"Now, children, what did we talk about in our last Sun-day School class?"
    "Moses."
    "And what did Moses do?"
    "He broke a calf."
    "He smashed a calf, but what else?"
                    —*Sunday School: Little Carr Creek*

"Shade hit him on the jaw with a fist, and him being a Christian he turned his cheek. That's Bible. And then Shade hit him on the other'n."   —*"Pee" Slone*

"The Devil is going wild trying to find people to do his meanness for him."

"Recollect that time you helped me move them mission-aries and their plunder in my truck from Hell-Each-Way in Morgan County to here on our creek? The road out of Hell was in the branch, run between two cliffs, and them close together, and we got stuck. Had to work the load over. The woman wore a flour sack dress and it read 'White Lily' front and back. I rented them a house and they turned out good neighbors. They'd come to Kentucky from South Dakota in the beginning. I reckon they'd already saved everybody out there and figured us heathen in Knott county needed religion worse than they did in Morgan."   —*Mal Gibson*

"When a preacher is a-preaching I want to hear it! I want to hear it a-ringing from one mountain to the other."   —*Frank Hicks*

"If you wanted to, you could be the pearl of God."

"All the preaching that's done for money hain't worth a pewter penny."

"I heard a preacher say they's infants in hell not a span long. I don't believe it. It's not in the Book. I want to know who told him? He hain't been there yet."

"When I was a soldier in the war we had the best chaplain ever was. He could cut your heart like nobody else. He could water your eyes. He could get down into your livings."

"We had a pretty meeting last Easter Sunday at Old Carr Churchhouse. Four preachers preached, and we had to sing down three of them."

"I'm not a Bible-read preacher. So I preach the best wise I can."

"The preacher I want to hear preach is one who is rooted and grounded in the Word."

"I wore my new earbobs I got for Christmas to church last Sunday and I got a whole big lot of compliments on them."
      "What did God say?"

"I'm expecting this old world to end any day now."

"Everything has to be right on the mark around him. When he gets to heaven, be it he ever does, and the Big Gate is open to let him in, he'll more'n likely say, 'Old Man, them hinges could use a drop of oil, my opinion.' "
—*Callie Hicks*

"Last Sunday I got out of bed and tuck me a drink of likker, and had my breakfast, and pretty soon I was off for Old Carr Church. I'd got in sight of the churchhouse when I bethought myself. I turned around and walked back home. I'll not sit in a congregation with whiskey on my breath. I've got that much principle."
—*Clay Collins*

"Live right in this life and you'll see pretty things in the next 'un."
—*Uncle Bill Maxey*

"Shore I traded in your store and bought some goods I never paid for. That was last year, back when I was 'lost.' I've joined the church since then and when God forgave me my sins he forgave my debts."

"You ever heard of Luther Burbank, the man who messes with plants? I have, and he's going to Hell when he dies. He changed the ice potato from what it used to be. There's Scripture against changing nature."

"I'm not a monkey, and I'm not akin to a monkey. The Bible says man was created in the image of the Lord, so He wasn't a monkey either."
—*Randy Grigsby*

"The Almighty retched down his hand and saved me from the Lake of Fire."

"Here was their brother come to see them. Come all the way from Bourbon County. He'll have to wait. They won't skip church. They have to first go down the creek and listen to that preacher. They've fed him so much fried chicken his belly is hanging out over his belt and he can't see his feet."

"When they forbid Noah Blevins from preaching at the Dry Springs Churchhouse, he said, 'If I was back in my young days, I'd let my 38-special do my talking for me.' "

"I know that a time will come when we all have to lay down our hoes forever, but until it comes for me I aim to keep on digging."

"There come in here some Mormons, the first Mormons to ever come in here. They were after believers their way. The one man they got to was Les' Rich', and he come over to them, and it was January and they broke ice in the creek and baptised him, and they baptised him without knowing his really name. They had to do it all over again when they found out, for when Les got to heaven He wouldn't know who Les was. They put him under again, and they done it right that time—Lester Arthur Richardson."

"I'd say it was along in the early 1960s I was talking to Old Tom Hagan on the street in Whitesburg when a stranger stepped up to us—he might of been a preacher—and he asked, "Could you gentlemen direct me to the Church of God?" Old Tom answered, "Well, now, let me see. The Methodist Church is down the street yonder on the left, and the Presbyterian Church is behind the courthouse, and the Baptist Church is across the railroad tracks. That's the lot of them. God ain't got no church in this town."   —*Venters Cornett*

"When I die I want a big funeral. I want people hollering and crying and taking on. I want to leave this world right."

 Yarns

"He can lay two cobs on the ground six inches apart, keep his hands in his pockets and talk them together.

He'll talk and the cobs will inch toward each other until they tip."

"Who told you that?"

"He did."

"Did you believe it?"

"Now, no."

"By that worm bucket I see you've been out on one of your fishing sprees. Don't start telling me about all them big'uns that got away."

"I'll come clean with you. I put out six lines and barely got a nibble. But if I had time for it I'd tell you about the huge catfish swallowing my boat."

"I'm in a hurry myself. What say you tell me along about December the thirty-second when we hain't doing nothing else?"   —*James Perry, Jr.*

"There's a record of a man here on this creek selling his soul to the Devil. I heard of it a long time ago. I wasn't more than a dozen years old. The way it was told to me was he was walking along one day and rocks began to rain down on him. After then wherever he went he walked in a shower of rocks. He had to wear a pot on his head to keep from having his brains knocked out. He knew from the start it was Old Scratch doing it. Finally he got tired of it and he spoke up to the Devil and said if he would stop the rocks he'd do what he wanted him to do. What the Devil wanted I wasn't told. After then when he entered a house the smoke started coming down the chimney back'ards, and the plates jumped off the table, and the chairs lined up and danced. This is what I heard as a child and it's something a body never forgets."   —*Bob Young*

"A horse trader tried to sell me a pony on Jockey Day and this is how swift he said it could run. He told me a rainstorm was coming up once and almost caught up with him. But not plumb. The pony ran so fast only half of the saddle got wet."

"Bristol Taylor used to tell of catching a mole in his ginseng patch and how he buried it alive to punish it. The joke was on whoever believed him."

"What's a man your age doing with them little holes on his cheeks—baby dimples?"
"When I was a tadwhacker I fell down on a corn stubble."
"But you've got one in each cheek."
"I fell down twice."

 Tales

"Old Sid Pridemore never went nowhere much in his life. Never traveled farther than the forks of Troublesome Creek to pay his taxes, and to set once on a jury. That was yonder when the creekbed was the road and you had to travel horseback, by wagon or shanks-mare.

"When final-last a road was built up Quicksand and an automobile could get in and out, Sid's son-in-law, John Zeek Smith, talked him into going with him to Hazard in Perry County. Going to let Sid see a speck of the world.

"Well, sir, they got to Hazard and old Sid's eyes were big as turnips. He kept saying. 'What's creation come to?' John Zeek drove into Hazard and was heading down the main street when he suddenly mashed on the brake and came to a full stop. Old Sid, he asked, 'What are ye quitting for?' And John Zeek he said, 'Don't you see that red light hanging overhead?' And Old Sid said, 'Why, go right on. We'll miss it fully ten feet.' "

"I'd pulled my truck off the road and was checking the tires when this long overgrown automobile pulled up beside me, and the driver was somebody I'd grown up with on Carr Creek and hadn't seen since Noah's flood. Away back yonder he'd moved up to Ohio, or somers, and I'd lost track of him. Up to the factories. He was in this big car with his woman and a bunch of young'uns. They were like chickens in a coop."

"I said, 'If I'd a-knowed you was coming I'd of cut my toenails.' And he said. 'You've got uglier than the last time I saw you. I'm a great mind to pick me up a sand rock and run you all the way back to Big Doubles where you belong.' Then I asked, 'Is all them young'uns yours?' "

"And he said, 'Yeah. Every last one. And I'm a-going to have eight more.' "

"That's when his woman stuck her head out of the car window and spoke up and said, 'He might have eight more by somebody else, but he ain't going to have 'em by me. I've done my do.' "   —*Mal Gibson*

"I'd swear to it. I haven't had a job in two years."

"Have you looked for one? They don't come searching for you."

"I tried to get on at the mine on Yellow Creek. And at Scratch Back. Pole City, too. They told me they're not taking on the younger men nowadays. Or the unmarried."

"Why's the reason?"

"Claim they don't show up on Mondays, and come in hungover on Tuesdays."

"What do you do with yourself from day to day? I'd go crazy with nothing to do."

"Ay, I just lay around the house. Anyhow, Maw is getting up in years and needs somebody on the place. Seventy-eight last month."

"Then I suppose you grew a master garden this spring. And a large patch of bread corn."

"Naw. Not much of a crop, or a garden either. Maw fell and broke her hip before she got much planted."

"Here I was twenty-three years old and couldn't hardly read and I got it in head to go back to school. What sort of a hereafter was there for me unless I jacked up my education? I'd heard of a boarding school over in Knott County run by a Mrs. Lloyd who didn't care who you was, or what you had, she'd take you in. I didn't even own a suitcase or a trunk or any clothes much to stuff in one. I packed my few duds in a coffee sack and tuck off. She did too, take me in. Mrs. Lloyd did. I was to work my board and tuition off in the carpenter shop. First, I built me a trunk. There I was in the third grade with a dozen or so little fellows in short pants and girls in ribbons and me old enough to have created any one of them.

"What the scholars done was nickname me 'Tall Corn.' The teasing didn't bother me. They'd say, 'Hey, up there! How's the weather?' Not one stood much above my knees. Walking in the play yard was like wading chickens. But I had trouble with my letters. Like, the word t-h-e read e-h-t. Come to find out, Mrs. Lloyd did, my eyes were picking up words backside front. Bassackards, as me and you would say. I couldn't do nothing about it, and Mrs. Lloyd couldn't do nothing but try, so I quit. I quit and hit for the house.

"The summer after that I was over in Ashcamp in Pike County looking for work in the mines and there wasn't no jobs, and I run into a fellow selling Bibles. He told me I could sell Bibles if I wanted to. He'd back me. All I had to do was to go to Nashville, Tennessee and take a week's training at the Southwestern Book Company. I told him I'd sell Bibles, or goose manure, whatever folks would pay money for. I was that low. He connected me with the book company and they sent me a train ticket against what I was going to earn, and within three weeks I'd put in the training in Nashville and was sent off with a buddy to Lee County, Mississippi.

"Square off, we rented us a room in a bungalow house in Tupelo, me and my buddy did. Our bed was a mattress and springs set up on wooden horses. As we were out on the road week days, we were never in Tupelo at the same time except Sundays. Who we rented from was a woman who said she couldn't hardly understand us. She said we spoke 'hill-billy.' We couldn't hardly understand her either. Her man run a print shop and always had some fun going. Big to joke and he told us some hot-dingers. Windy as a March day.

"We divided the county between us. We thumped a nickel heads-or-tails and I drew the east side—the side you have to walk a mile to cross a swamp to get out of town. It was hot. July. Dusty. The ground scorched your feet through your soles. This was cotton country and the crops laid by and the farmers resting under china-berry trees and eating watermelons and peeling peaches and with all the time in the world to listen to a Bible spiel. Well, s'r, I wasn't getting rich, or doing too bad either, until a thing happened.

"One day I stopped at a country house and pecked on the screen door and a woman came to it a-wiping her hands on her apron. She said she was into making fig preserves and didn't have time to mess with me, and if I wanted to sell something I'd have to talk to her husband. I didn't see her man nowhere so I asked after him and she said the last time she'd seen him he was heading toward the barn with a coil of rope on his arm and that had been fully two hours ago.

"They'd taught me in Nashville not to let a probable customer slip through my fingers so I headed to the cow lot, and through it to the barn. The barn doors were closed and latched from the inside. I poked a stick through a crack and lifted the latch and swung open one of the doors and there hung a man from a rafter with a rope around his neck. Dead as a doorknob.

"The word got out and everybody learnt about the suicide and about me discovering it. Everybody in Lee County. Even over in Itawamba County where I strayed sometimes and wasn't supposed to. Not my territory. Who ever saw a county line? Let me climb onto a verandah and open my sample case than they'd quick yap, 'Oh, you're the one who found the man hanging in the barn! Tell us about it.' That's all they wanted to hear. What did I know? No nothing. Back in Tupelo on Sundays, smart asses would step up to me and crack 'What about that man committing sewer pipe!' That got old quick. My sales fell off three quarters.

"My buddy peddling on the west side of the county wasn't having any trouble. Doing all right. I told the husband of the woman who rented to us about it and he figured out a remedy to fit the situation. He printed me up some cards, calling card size, and when somebody started that stuff, 'Oh, you're the man who—' I'd hand them a card. After then my business picked back up. The card read: 'I don't know a damn thing about it.' "

"Have you heard about my accident? You hain't? Bad news don't travel as fast as it used to. This youngest boy of mine was driving and he tried to make an airplane out of the car and we went over a bank. Mashed my head in and hurt my leg bad. My own flesh and blood done this to his mother.

"I stayed in the hospital three days and two nights and that was all I could stand. The food, a dog wouldn't eat. I told the doctor I was leaving and he said, 'You mustn't. You're not ready to put weight on that hame leg.' And I said, 'I'm going if I have to crawl.' And I said, 'Being you've done something for me, I want to do something for you, and for everybody else in this hospital before I leave. Roll me to the kitchen and let me fix you and the patients a meal worth eating. Your cooks don't know 'taters from horse apples.' "   —*Sylvia Turner*

"The story my father used to tell was of when he was a boy in Jenkins, Kentucky, along about 1920 to '23. He and a few friends decided to pick some apples from a tree owned by 'Bad John' Wright, who was known and feared far and wide as a man who had no reluctance about putting someone in the grave. He supposedly had killed many a man. My father remembers having seen one lying in a ditch. In those days, he said you could openly wear a holster. Well, anyway, as the boys were picking apples, against their better judgment, along comes Bad John. Seeing him coming up the road all the boys ran off except my father. As he stood there trembling in his shoes, Mr. Wright stood over him and in a powerful voice asked if my father and the boys had been picking apples. My father, too afraid to lie, said they were. Just as he thought he was going to be shot on the spot, Bad John broke into a broad smile, and said it was O.K., but just to ask him first next time, and then handed my dad an apple and told him to get along.

"Well, my father was so impressed with this incident that I believe it influenced his dealings with people all his life."   —*Bruce Acciavatti (letter)*

"We sort of left Kentucky and strode off down to Florida. The reason I decided to leave was I had ten children, most of them girls, and girls can give you trouble. They were going wild. My boys, too, they were getting mean-er'n the Devil. I had to move my family out of there. Another cause, the mines were down and I couldn't feed them. When I could get a job it was on my knees underground digging coal. Brute work. Dangerous. My brother was killed in the mines.

"What I done was to take the two oldest girls and the two oldest boys and headed off hitchhiking to Florida. I aimed for us to go down and pick oranges. I started with six cents in my pocket and along the way I spent it on a cigar. We are all smokers. I crumbled it into paper wrappers and made us all a cigarette apiece.

"We caught rides, long ones and short ones, in trucks. Cars wouldn't pick us up. Rode mostly in empty fruit trucks traveling south. We had one long ride, the main one, from Tennessee and all the way across Georgia and on to Lake City, Florida. Took a whole day. Up in the cab the driver and his helper had food to eat, and we didn't. Every once in a while they'd throw back something to us, like feeding dogs. We were glad to get it but it hurt our feelings.

"Finally we made it to Sumpter County, to the orchards. We found work right off and pitched in. We pulled oranges or grapefruit all day and packed crates half the night. Took just two weeks to raise enough money to hire a truck to go back home and bring down the rest of the family.

"That was eighteen years ago and since then we've seen good times and we've seen some bad'uns. Several of my children growed up and moved back to Kentucky. Kentucky was in them.

"Up there where we used to live in the head of Carr Creek there are a lot of Gibsons. There is, or was, another Amos Gibson. A different set from us. We're no kin. My daddy was Harve Gibson, from over on Bullskin in Perry County.

"Ay, law. Eighteen years! Time's a-moving on."

—*Amos Gibson, Bushnell, Florida*

"We lived on Dry Fork in Letcher County and I was ten years old, and there was to be a pie supper on Saturday night at the schoolhouse in the head of the hollow, and I wanted to go, and my pap finally let me, and there was this girl I wanted to get with, and I aimed to buy her pie but it went for two dollars and I couldn't top that, and when it was over everybody got gone except one boy, and he said, 'I reckon you'll have to go home with me,' and I did, and we couldn't see the path it was so dark and we had to walk in the branch to find our way, and we got our feet wet, and we went into his house, a log house, and everybody was asleep, and me and him climbed a ladder to the loft and slept between two feather beds, and next morning we came down the ladder and his mommy cooked some mush for us, for cornmeal was all they had, and we ate that, and when I got back to my house my pap asked where I'd stayed and I told him, and he said, 'Them folks don't have nothing.' "

—*Bruce Taylor*

"Bob Hall has the credit for introducing baloney into Perry County. His store was so small all he had on the shelves was a box of crackers, a jar of mayonnaise, and a roll of baloney, and only one customer could get into his store at a time. Or, that's how we'd tell it and laugh about it. But what I'm going to tell you is what Bob Hall told me about Asher McGuire. One day Bob went into Asher McGuire's place and there was Asher with his shoes off, reared back in a chair, and with bandaged feet up on a table. He asked Asher 'What happened?' Asher explained that he'd got it into his head to go on an excursion train to a Reds' baseball game in Cincinnati. And he'd bought himself a new pair of shoes to wear. When the train arrived in Cincinnati, Asher started walking toward where he thought the ball field was, and he walked, and he walked, and he walked. He never found it. After walking a couple of hours he had to turn back to catch the excursion train home. So that was what happened to his feet. Anyhow, he'd broken-in the new shoes."   —*Jim Bergman*

"My mother suffered terrible from a pain in her cheek, a pain so strong it would nearly take her life. Pills wouldn't knock it and the doctors couldn't cure it. We'd heard of a healer so we took her to him. A two-day trip, going and coming. That was back in the '20s. We hitched up a pair of mules to a wagon and put in food and quilts and fodder and rode to Letcher County, and on across Pine Mountain, and on past bad Branch, nearly to the Virginia line where the healer lived. His woman didn't want him to do it but he done it anyway. He come out to the wagon and said something to my mother, and touched her cheek, or something. He done something to my mother, I don't know what. We headed back home and my mother never had another attack as long as she lived. She lived to be way up there."
                                                    —*Sam Stamper*

 Chewing the Cud

Chewing My Cud
   I sparked an old maid, kissed her twice;
   Her lips were dry but they sufficed.

   I bought a rude cow, she milked water;
   She kicked me where she shouldn't have oughta.

Skin your eyes and see the fishes;
Shake a money tree if you crave riches.

"When I was a tadwhacker, not old enough to make a
shuck rattle when I peed, I learnt a verse off somebody.
I'd say it just to act smart and grown up although I
didn't know what it meant. And I don't know now.
Maybe I didn't hear it right.

"Up jumped a six-foot fellow,
And he was a fighter;
I up with a lump o' coal
And knocked him in the bugle,
Knocked him into the soup pot
A'biling in the kitchen.
   Ah, law me.
And I say myself a'witching,
Saw me a pretty girl
A'cooking in the kitchen.
Link fol day, my doody and yea."

—*Woodrow Amburgey*

"Paint my boots and set'em
      on the bench,
I'm going to Jellico to
      see Suzy Hanks.
Holler-ding, baby.
Holler-ding.

"Old grey goose went down
      to the river.
If I'd been a gander I'd
      of gone with her.
Holler-ding, baby.
Holler-ding."   —*As sung by Colones Nickols (1933)*

Big Dates

In seventeen hundred and seventy-three
"D. Boon cilled a bar" in a sycamine tree.

During the Revolution, his hair in a bow,
G. Washington crossed the Delaware in a batteau.

In eighteen something, during a cold snap,
D. Crockett invented the coonskin cap.

By the middle of the century Johnny Appleseed
With a pot on his head had the wilderness treed.

In humpteen-hundred, after a visit to his keg,
Some coot or other used the first Sexton peg.

In nineteen-eighteen Old Kaiser Bill
Swallowed an American rifle pill.

In forty-one Schickelgruber should have known
He couldn't both the world and Kentucky take on.

Jockey Day Calls

"Round and sound, slick as a mole;
Two good eyes and heavy in foal.

"Round and sound, tough as a whang;
Two good eyes and four in the spring."

School butter, chicken flutter,
Rotten eggs for teacher's supper.

Teacher's pick got awful wet;
How'd the bucket get upset?

Got a thrashing, was it fair?
Spied a louse in Lucy's hair.

Teacher thought my hide was peeling,
My patched pants spared me the feeling.

Up the poplar, down the oak,
Was expelled at a stroke.

Got my schooling, at one crack,
In the front door, out the back.

"Old John Shell, Kentucky's oldest man,
How come you're the eldest in the land?"
"I ate cornbread and soupbeans,
Drank mountain dew in between."
"Why did you never grow a beard?"
"Of nesting mice I was afeared."
"What song shall we sing
The day you kick the bucket?"
"Take me back to Ole Kentuckett."

—*John Shell (1812?–1922)*

"Knives and forks,
Plates and tumblers,
All school teachers
Are hard numbers."

Old Prentice Hogan never took a bath,
He smelled like a squirrel—a squirrel and a calf.
As a snake slips its skin, an ant sheds its wings,
Old Prentice's hide peeled off pretty in the spring.

"A short horse is soon curried,
A dead cat is soon buried,
A bad debt is long carried."

"Slop the shoat, shoe the mare,
Wash your face, comb your hair,
Join the army.
Sign for navy,
Keep your sleeves
Out of the gravy."

Knife Trader

You call that thing a knife? A pocket knife?
Sort of does look like one.
Open her up, let me check the blades.
Call them blades? Son of a beagle!
They wouldn't cut hot butter on a summer's day.
A grandaddy Boker, huh? Who told you that?
Handed down in the family, aye?
Genuine article, asking a hundred dollars?
Uh-uh. Don't try pulling that hockey on me.
I've been swapping knives sixty-five years,
I've heard all the tales and everything that follows.
You look like a fellow who could use two bucks,
And even at that I'm paying a lot.
Maybe I can sharpen the scudder a whet,
And squeeze a little Three-in-One along the joints,
And put it off on some witty with no more gumption
    than a baby,
And get my money back.
Just maybe.

Creeks I've Lived On
Mad Calf, Mad Calf
Born and bred;
Strong in the arm,
Woolly in the head.

I never aimed
To go to pot;
I moved around
An awful lot.

Endured a spell
On Hell-Each-Way,
Then the devil
Was to pay.

I dwelt on Frozen,
And then at Ice;
Came within a hair
Of freezing twice.

I tried Dry Creek,
That wouldn't do.
What did folk drink?
Mountain dew!

Moved to Crooked Creek,
Gee-o, what a mess!
I couldn't live honest
Doing my best.

Moved up Stinking
As far as she goes,
Lived with a clothespin
Pinching my nose.

I bought on Sporty,
Thought I'd have fun;
Tee-total worse thing
Ever I done.

I moved back to Mad Calf—
End of the line;
Now I'm faring
Sassy and fine.

Truck Driver

My name is Mack.
It's printed on my cap.
What did you figure:
Toro, Peterbilt, Coors?
I see "K.M.I" on yours,
And what does that mean—
"Kentucky Mental Institute?"
By the hang of your jaw there's no dispute.
Damn, you're touchy! Working up a heat.
Hell, Old Son, I'd as soon fight as to eat.
But I need to shove on to Atlanta,
Can't blow a minute on fists or banter,
Got to get my rig rolling, no time for foes,
And coming from Big Mack that's no lie,
So bye-bye, Bozo—I mean K.M.I.—,
Don't go sticking no beans up your nose.

I LOVE MY ROOSTER

We lived in Houndshell mine camp the year of the coal boom, and I remember the mines worked three shifts a day. The conveyors barely ceased their rusty groaning for five months. I recollect the plenty there was, and the silver dollars rattling wherever men walked; and I recollect the goldfinches stayed that winter through, their yellow breasts turning mole-gray.

We were eating supper on a November evening when Sim Brannon, the foreman, came to tell Father of the boom. Word came that sudden. Father talked alone with Sim in the front room, coming back to the kitchen after a spell. A chuckle of joy broke in his throat as he sat down at the table again, swinging the baby off the floor onto his knee. He reached for the bowl of shucky beans, shaping a hill of them on his plate with a spoon. Never had he let us play with victuals. "They've tuck the peg off o' coal," he said. "Government's pulled the price tag. Coal will be selling hand over fist."

The baby stuck a finger into the bean mound. Father didn't scold. Mother lifted the coffeepot, shaking the spout clear of grounds. "I never heard tell it had a peg," she said.

Fern and Lark and I looked at Father, wondering what a coal peg was. The baby's face was bright and wise, as if he knew.

Father thumped the table, marking his words. "I say it's ontelling what a ton o' coal will sell for. They's a lack afar north at the big lakes, and in countries across the waters. I figure the price will double or treble." He lifted a hand over the baby's head. "Yon blue sky might be the limit."

Our heads turned toward the window. We saw only the night sky, dark as gob smoke.

Mother set the coffeepot down, for it began to tremble in her hand. She thrust a stick of wood into the stove, though supper was done and the room warm. "Will there be plenty in the camps?" she asked, uncertain.

Father laughed, spoon in air. "Best times ever hit this country," he said, jarring the table. "Why, I'm a-liable to draw twice the pay I get now." He paused, staring at us. We sat as under a charm, listening. "We're going to feed these chaps till they're fat as mud," he went on. "Going to put proper clothes on their backs and buy them a few pretties. We'll live like folks were born to live. This hardscrabble skimping I'm tired of. We're going to fare well."

The baby made a cluck with his tongue, trying to talk. He squeezed a handful of beans until they popped between his fingers.

"For one thing," Father said, "I'm going to buy me a pair o' high-top boots. These clodhoppers I'm wearing have wore a half acre o' bark off my heels."

The cracked lids of the stove began to wink. Heat grew in the room.

"I want me a fact'ry dress," Fern spoke.

"I need me a shirt," I said. "A boughten shirt. And I want a game rooster. One that'll stand on my shoulder and crow."

Father glanced at me, suddenly angry.

"Me," Lark began, "I want—" But he could not think what he wanted most of all.

"A game rooster!" Father exclaimed. "They's too many gamble cocks in this camp already. Why, I'd a'soon buy you a pair o' dice and a card deck. I'd a'soon."

"A pet rooster wouldn't harm a hair," I said, the words small and stubborn in my throat. And I thought of one-eyed Fedder Mott, who oft played mumbly-peg with me, and who went to the rooster matches at the Hack. Fedder would tell of the fights, his eye patch shaking, and I would wonder what there was behind the patch. I'd always longed to spy.

"No harm, as I see, in a pet chicken," Mother said.

"I want me a banty," Lark said.

Father grinned, his anger gone. He batted an eye at Mother. "We hain't going into the fowl business," he said. "That's for shore." He gave the baby a spoonful of beans. "While ago I smelled fish on Sim Brannon—fried salt fish he'd just et for supper. I'm a-mind to buy a whole wooden kit o' mackerel. We'll be able."

Mother raised the window a grain, yet it seemed no less hot. She sat down at the foot of the table. The baby jumped on Father's knee, reaching arms toward her. His lips rounded, quivering to speak. A bird sound came out of his mouth.

"I bet he wants a pretty-piece bought for him," Fern said.

"By juckers," Father said, "if they was a trinket would larn him to talk, I'd buy it." He balanced the baby in the palm of a hand and held him straight out, showing his strength. Then he keened his eyes at Mother. "You hain't said what you want. All's had their say except you."

Mother stared into her plate. She studied the wedge print there. She did not lift her eyes.

"Come riddle, come riddle," Father said impatiently.

"The thing I want hain't a sudden idea," Mother said quietly. Her voice seemed to come from a long way off. "My notion has followed me through all the coal camps we've lived in, a season here, a span there, forever moving. Allus I've aimed to have a house built on the acres we heired on Shoal Creek o' Troublesome. Fifteen square acres we'd have to raise our chaps proper. Garden patches to grow victuals. Elbowroom a-plenty. Fair times and bad, we'd have a roof-tree. Now, could we save half you make, we'd have enough money in time."

"Half?" Father questioned. "Why, we're going to start living like folks. Fitten clothes on our backs, food a body can enjoy." He shucked his coat, for he sat nearest the stove. He wiped sweat beads off his forehead.

"I need me a shirt," I said. "A store-bought shirt." More than a game rooster, more than anything, I wanted a shirt made like a man's. Being eight years old, I was ashamed to wear the ones Mother sewed without tails to stuff inside my breeches.

"No use living barebones in the midst o' plenty," Father said. "Half is too much."

Mother rose from the table and leaned over the stove. She looked inside to see if anything had been left to burn. She tilted the coffee pot, making sure it hadn't boiled dry. "Where there's a boom one place," she said, "there's bound to be a famine in another. Coal gone high, and folks not able to pay." Her lips trembled. "Fires gone out. Chaps chill and sick the world over withouten a roof above their heads." She picked up the poker, lifted a stove cap, and shook the embers. Drops of water began to fry on the stove. She was crying.

"Be-grabbies!" Father said. "Stop poking that fire! This room's already hot as a ginger mill."

On a Saturday afternoon Father brought his two-week pay pocket home, the first since the boom. He came into the kitchen, holding it aloft, unopened. Mother was cooking a skillet of meal mush and the air was heavy with the good smell. I was in haste to eat and go, having promised Fedder Mott to meet him at the schoolhouse gate. Fedder and I planned to climb the mine tipple.

"Corn in the hopper and meal in the sack," Father said, rattling the pocket.

He let Fern and Lark push fingers against it, feeling the greenbacks inside; and he gave it to the baby to play with upon the floor, watching out of the tail of his eye. Mother was uneasy with Father's carelessness. The baby opened his mouth, clucking, churring. He made a sound like a wren setting a nest of eggs.

"Money, money," Fern said, trying to teach him.

He twisted his lips, his tongue straining. But he could not speak a word.

"I'd give every red cent to hear him say one thing," Father said.

The pay pocket was opened, the greenbacks spread upon the table. We had never seen such a bounty. Father began to figure slowly with fingers and lips. Fern counted swiftly. She could count nearly as fast as the Houndshell schoolteacher.

Father paused, watching Fern. "This chap can out-count a check-weigh-man," he bragged.

"Sixty-two dollars and thirty cents," Fern announced, and it was right, for Mother had counted too. "Wisht I had me a fact'ry dress," Fern said.

"I want a shirt hain't allus a-gaping at the top o' my breeches," I said.

Father wrinkled his forehead. "These chaps need clothes, I reckon. And I've got my fancy set on a pair o' boots. They's no use going about like ragglee-taggle gypsies with money in hand. We're able to live decent."

"Socks and stockings I've knit," Mother said, "and shirts and dress garments I've sewed a-plenty for winter. They hain't made by store pattern, but they'll wear and keep a body warm. Now, I'm willing to do without and live hard to build a homeplace."

"Oh, I'm willing, too," Father complained, "but a man likes to get his grunt and groan in." He gathered the greenbacks, handing them to Mother. He stacked the three dimes. "Now, if I wasn't allus seeing the money, I could save without hurt. Once hit touches my sight and pocket, I'm afire. I burn to spend."

Mother rolled the bills. She thrust them into an empty draw sack, stowing all in her bosom. "One thing you could do," she told Father, "but it's not for me to say do, or not do. If you was a-mind, you could bring the pay pockets home unopened. We'd not think to save just half. I'd save all we could bear, spend what was needed. You'd not see the spark of a dime till we got enough for a house. I say this boom can't last eternal."

Father pulled his eyebrows, deciding. The baby watched. How like a bird he cocked his head. "Oh, I'm a-mind," Father said at last, "but the children ought to have a few coins to pleasure themselves with. A nickel a week."

"I want mine broke in pennies," Lark called.

Fern counted swiftly, speaking in dismay, "It would take me nigh a year to save enough for an ordered dress."

"We'll not lack comfort nor pleasure," Mother promised. "Nor will we waste. The chaps can have the nickel. You get a pair o' boots—a pair not too costy. And we'll buy a kit o' fish."

She stirred butter into the meal mush, and it was done. Fern hurried dishes upon the table.

"The pair my head was set on cost eighteen dollars. Got toes so sharp you could kick a blacksnake's eye out. Reckon I'll just make these clodbusters I got on do."

"Them boots must o' been sprigged with gold tacks."

A buttery steam rose from our plates. We dipped up spoonfuls of mush; we scraped our dishes, pushing them back for more.

"Hit's good to see no biled leather breeches on the table for once," Father said. He blew on a spoon of mush to cool it for the baby. "Right today I'll buy that kit o' fish."

"They're liable to draw every cat in Houndshell Holler. Better you plug the cat hole in the back door first."

I slid from the table bench, pulling my hat off a peg.

"Where are you traipsing to?" Father asked.

"Going to play with Fedder Mott. He's yonder in the schoolyard."

"I know Fedder Mott," Lark spoke, gulping much. "He's a boy jist got one eyeball."

I ran the Houndshell road. A banjo twanged among the houses. A hundred smokes stirred in chimney pots, rising, threading chilly air. I reached the schoolhouse, breathing hard, and Fedder Mott was swinging on the gate. He jumped down.

"I'd nigh give you out," he said, his blue eye wide.

I said, "If my pap knowed about the tipple, I'd not got to come."

Fedder leaned against the fence. He was a full head taller than I, a year older. He drew a whack of tobacco from a hind pocket, bit a squirrely bite, and offered the cut to me.

I shook my head.

He puckered his lips, speaking around the wad in his jaw. "They hain't nothing worth seeing in that tipple tower. I done climbed thar." He waited, champing teeth into the wad, making juice to spit. "I'd figured we'd go to the rooster fight. Now you've come too late."

"Was I to go," I said, "my pap would tear up stakes."

Two children ran by, playing tag-o. A man came walking the road. Fedder spat into a rut. The black patch trembled on his face. It was like a great dark eye, dwarfing the blue one. I looked at it curiously.

"Afore long, fellers will be coming down from the Hack," Fedder said. "We'll larn which roosters whooped."

I studied the eye patch. It was the size of a silver dollar, hanging by a string looped around his head. What lay behind it? Was there a hole square into his skull? I was almost ashamed to ask, almost afraid. I drew a circle on the ground with my shoe, measuring the words: "I'll go to the rooster fight sometime, if one thing—"

"If'n what?"

"If you'll let me see your eye pocket."

Fedder blew the tobacco cud across the road. He pushed the long tails of his shirt inside his breeches. "You'll spy and won't go."

"'F'ad die."

We saw a man walking the path off the ridge, coming toward us from the Hack. He came fast, though he was still too distant to be named. We watched him wind the crooked path and be lost among the houses.

"Ag'in' we go to the cockpit," Fedder said, "I'll let you look."

"I choose now."

Fedder stood firm. "Ag'in' that time, I will." He hushed a moment, listening for the man who came from the ridge. "Afore long I'll not be wearing this patch," he said. "I've heared o' glass eyeballs. Hit's truth. They say even a hound dog wears one in Anvers camp. Five round dollars they cost, and could I grab a holt on that much, I'd git the schoolteacher to mail an order."

"Won't your pap buy you a glass 'un?"

"If'n I was a flycatcher, he wouldn't feed me gnats."

"I'm going to save money, come every week. I've got me something in my head to buy."

"Hit reads in a magazine where a feller kin sell garden seeds and make a profit. A hundred packages o' squash and dill and turnip sold, and I'd have me enough."

We saw the man afar off on the road. He was heading our way, walking a hippety-hop on short legs.

"Bulger Hyden," Fedder said.

Fedder hailed him as he reached the schoolhouse gate, and he stopped. He shed his coat, being warm from haste, and he wore a green-dotted shirt.

"Who whooped?" Fedder asked.

Bulger Hyden's face grew wrinkled as a doty mushroom; he swung his arms emptily, glancing at the sky's promise of weather. There was a hint of snow. Goldfinches blew over us like leaves, piping their dry winter song above the conveyor's ceaseless rattle.

"Steph Harben's Red Pyle rimwrecked my Duckwing," Bulger grumbled. "Steph fotched that bird from West Virginia and scratches in all the money. I say it hain't fair pitting a furren cock." He folded his coat, balancing it on an elbow crotch, making ready to go. "I thought a sight o' my little Duckwing." His voice hoarsened. "I cherished that rooster." And he went on, and I looked after him, thinking a green-speckled shirt was the choicest garment ever a fellow could wear.

Winter came before I could go to the Hack. Snow fell late in November and scarcely left the ground for two months. The rooster fights were halted until spring. I recollect the living river of wind pouring down Houndshell Hollow. For bird and varmint, and, I hear, for folk beyond the camps, it was a lean time. But miners fared well. I recollect the warm linsey coats, the red woolen gloves, the high-top boots; I recollect full pokes of food going into houses, the smell of cooking victuals. Children wore store clothes. They bought spin-tops and pretties at the commissary. Boys' pockets clinked money. Only Fedder Mott and I had to wind our own balls and whittle our tops. I hoarded the nickels Mother gave me, telling Fedder I might buy a shirt when enough had been saved. Fedder never had a penny. He spoke bitterly of it. "My pap wouldn't plait me shucks if'n I was a chair bottom." And he said, "I hear tell hit's might' nigh the same with yore pap. Hit's told the eagle squalls when he looses a dollar."

Mother spent little. We hardly dared complain, having already more than we had known before. Once, in January, Father tried to figure the amount of money Mother had stored in the draw sack. He marked with a stub pencil, and Mother watched. At last he let the baby have the pencil. "My wage has riz three times," he said hopelessly, "though I don't know how much. Why, fellers tell me they're getting twelve and fifteen dollars a day. Deat Sheldon claims he made twenty dollars, four days handrunning, but he works a fold in the gravy tunnel and can load standing up."

"I've no idea o' the sum we've got," Mother said. "I opened one pay pocket and we're living out of it. The rest I've kept sealed."

"How's a body to know when a plenty's been saved? I hain't in a notion yet setting aside for tombstone and coffin box. Fellers in the mines 'gin to say the buffalo bellows when I spend a nickel."

"If you long for a thing enough, you'll give up for it. You'll sacrifice. The coal famine is bound to end some day. Come that time, we'll fit the house to the money."

Father began to tease. "What say we count the greenbacks? My curiosity is being et raw."

"Now, no. Hit would be a temptation to spend."

The baby sat up, threshing the air, puckering his lips. We looked, and he had bitten the rubber tip off the pencil.

"Hain't he old enough to be saying words?" Father asked.

"He talked to a cat once," Lark said. "I heared him."

"Ah, now," Mother chided. "Just a sound he made. Cats follow stealing in since we bought salt fish. Can't keep the cat hole plugged."

"He said 'kigid.' "

"That hain't a word," Fern said.

Father poked a finger at the baby, "By gollyard, if he'd just speak one word!"

The baby lifted his arms, mouth wide, neck stretched. He crowed.

"Thar's your rooster," Father chuckled, setting his eyes on me.

"I aim to own a real gamer," I bragged, irked by Father's teasing. "I aim to." I spoke without hope, not knowing that by spring it would come true.

"A good thing to have this double zero weather," Father drawled. "Hit driv the poker players and fowl gamblers indoors. But fellers claim that when the weather mends they'll be rooster fights in the Hack three days a week. Hit's high-low-jack and them fools lose every button cent."

Mother searched the baby's mouth for the pencil tip. "I call this boom a gamble," she said. "It's bound to end." She didn't find the rubber tip, for the baby had swallowed it down.

I told Fedder of Mother's prophecy as we sat by a fire on the creek bank. We had fish-hooks in an ice hole.

"Be-hopes the boom lasts till I git me a glass eye," he said. "My mind's set on it. I'd better have a batch o' garden seeds ordered and start selling."

"You couldn't stick a pickax in the ground, it's so froze," I told him. "Folks haven't a notion to buy seeds now."

Fedder rubbed his hands over the blaze, blowing a foggy breath. "I say winter hain't going to last forever neither."

I recollect thinking the long cold spell would never end. January diddled, and February crawled. March warmed a bit, thawing. The breasts of gold finches turned yellow as rubbed gold again. Fedder got his seeds, though when he should have been peddling them he'd climb the ridge to the rooster fights. Oft when a rooster was killed they'd let him bring the dead fowl home. Father forbade my going to the Hack; he put his foot down. But next to seeing was Fedder's telling. I came to know the names of the bravest cocks. I knew their markings, and the way they fought.

Fedder whistled for me one Thursday evening at the edge of dark. I heard and went outside, knowing his Kentucky redbird call. He stood beyond the fence with a coffee sack bundled in his arms; and he seemed fearful and anxious, and yet proud. His blue eye was wide, and the black patch had a living look. Packages of seeds rattled in his pockets.

"How much money have you mized?" he asked. "How much?" His voice was a husky whisper.

I guessed what the bundle held, scarcely daring to believe. I grew feverish with wonder.

"Eleven nickels," I said. "I couldn't save all."

The coffee sack moved; something threshed inside. A fowl's wing struck its thighs.

"I'm a-mind to sell you half ownership in my rooster," he said. "I will for yore eleven nickels, and if you'll keep him till I find a place. My pap would wring hits neck if I tuck him home."

I touched the bundle. My hand trembled. I shook with joy. "I been saving to buy a shirt," I said. "I want me a boughten shirt."

"You couldn't save enough by Kingdom Come. Eleven nickels, and jist you pen him. We'll halvers."

"Who'd he belong to?"

"Fotch the money. All's got to be helt a secret."

I brought my tocacco-sack bank and Father's mine lamp. We stole under the house, penning the rooster in a hen-coop. Father's voice droned over us in the kitchen. Fedder lit the lamp to count the money. The rooster stood blinking, red-eyed, alert. His shoulders were white, redding at the wing bows. Blood beads tipped his hackle feathers. His spurs were trimmed to fit gaffs. It was Steph Harben's Red Pyle.

"How'd you come by him?" I insisted.

"He fit Ebo, the black Cuban, and got stumped. He keeled down. They was a cut in his throat and you'd a-thought him knob dead. Steph gave him to me, and ere I reached the camp, he come alive. That thar cut was jist a scratch."

We crawled from beneath the house. Fedder smothered the light. "Don't breathe this to a soul," he warned. "Steph would auger to git him back, and my pap would throw duck fits. Now, you bring him to the schoolhouse ag'in' two o'clock tomorrow."

He moved toward the gate, the nickels ringing in his pocket. I went into the house and sat quietly behind the stove, feeling lost without my money, though recompensed by the rooster.

Father spoke, trotting the baby to Burnham Bright on a foot. "Warm weather's come," he mused. "Seems to me the Houndshell company ought to pare down on mining. Two days ago they hired four new miners, fellers from away yander."

"I know a boy come from Alabamy," Lark said. "I bet he's from yon side the waters."

"It's United States, America," Fern said.

"Sim Brannon believes something's bound to crack before long," Father went on. "Says hit's liable to come sudden. I'm in hopes my job don't split off."

"Come that time," Mother said, "maybe we'll have plenty saved for a house."

Father reached the baby to Mother. "I'm going to bed early," he yawned. "Last night I never got sixty winkles o' sleep. I reckon every tomcat in this camp was miaowing on the back porch."

"The fish draws 'um."

"A tinker man tapped on the door yesterday," Fern said, "and a big nanny cat ran in betwixt his legs."

"Hit's the one baby talked a word to," Lark said.

Father stretched sleepily. "I'm afeared the baby's a mute," he said. He set his chair aside. "The only thing that'd keep me awake this night would be counting the money we've got stacked away."

I waited at the schoolhouse gate, holding the rooster by the shanks. He snuggled against my jump jacket, pecking at the buttons. He stuck his head in my jacket pocket to see what was there. After a spell Fedder came, his eye patch trembling and the garden seeds as noisy upon him as grass crickets.

"Why'n't you kiver him?" he asked crossly. "He might a-been seen."

"He flopped the coffee sack off," I said. "Anyhow, he's been seen already. Crowed this morning before blue daylight and woke my pap. If I hadn't cried like gall, he'd been killed. Now it's your turn to keep."

Fedder bit a chew of tobacco, bit it with long front teeth as a squirrel bites. He spat into the road and looked up and down. "If I tuck him to my house, he'd be in the skillet by dinner." He closed his eye to think, and there was only the black patch staring. "I figure Steph Harben will buy him back. He's yon side the commissary, playing draughts. Air you of a notion?"

The cock lifted his head, poising it left and right. I loosed my hold about his legs and stroked his bright saddle. He sat on my arm.

"This rooster's a pet," I said. "When I tuck him out o' the coop, he jumped square onto my shoulder and crowed. I'm taking a liking to him."

"I jist lack selling fourteen seed papers gitting my eyeball. Never could I sell dills and rutabagas. If Steph will buy the rest, I'll rid my part. We got nowheres earthy to store a chicken."

"I hain't a-mind to sell."

Fedder packed the ground where he stood. The seeds rattled. The rooster pricked his head.

"You stay here till I git Steph," Fedder said. He swung around. "You stay."

He went in haste, and suddenly a great silence fell in the camp. The coal conveyor at the mines had stopped. Men stood at the drift mouth and looked down upon the rooftops. It was so still I could hear the far *per-chic-o-ree* of finches. I held the rooster at arm's length, wishing him free as a bird. I half hoped he would fly away. I set him on the fence, but he hopped to my shoulder and shook his wattles.

Back along the road came Fedder. Steph Harben hastened with him, wearing a shirt like striped candy, and never a man wore a finer one. The shirt was thinny—so thin that when he stood before me I could see the paddles of his collarbones.

Fedder said, "I've sold my part. Hit's you two trading."

Steph said, "Name yore price. Name."

I gathered the fowl in my arms. "I hain't a-mind to sell," I said.

We turned to stare at miners passing, going home long before quitting time, their cap lamps burning in broad day.

Steph was anxious. "Why hain't you willing?" he asked. "Name."

I dug my toe into the ground, scuffing dirt. "I love my rooster," I said. But I looked at Steph's shirt. It was very beautiful.

"If'n you'll sell," Fedder promised, "I'll let you spy at my eye pocket. Now, while it's thar, you kin look. Afore long I'll have a glass 'un."

I kicked a clod into the road. "I'll swap my part o' the rooster for that striped shirt. It can be cut down to fit."

"Shuck it off," Fedder told Steph.

Steph unbuttoned the shirt, slipped it over the blades of his shoulders, and handed it to me in a wad. He snatched the rooster, lighting out for home, and miners along the road glared at his bare back.

Fedder brushed his hat aside, catching the eye patch between forefinger and thumb. I was suddenly afraid, suddenly having no wish to see.

The patch was lifted. I looked, stepping back, squeezing the shirt into a ball. I turned, running, running with this sight burnt upon my mind.

I ran all the way home, going into the kitchen door as Father went, not staying the sow cat that stole in between my legs. Mother sat at the table, a pile of greenbacks before her, the empty pay pockets crumpled.

"Hell's bangers!" Father gasped, dropping heavily upon a chair and lifting the baby to his knee; and when he could speak above his wonder, "The boom's busted. I've got no job." But he laughed, and Mother smiled.

"I've heard already," Mother said. She laid a hand upon the money bills, flicking them under a thumb like a deck of gamble cards. "There's enough here to build a house, a house with windows looking out o' every room. And a grain left for a pair o' costy boots, a boughten shirt, a fac-t'ry dress, a few pretties."

The baby opened his mouth, curling his lips, pointing a stub finger. He pointed at the old nanny smelling the fish kit.

"Cat!" he said, big as life.

HERITAGE

I shall not leave these prisoning hills
Though they topple their barren heads to level earth
And the forests slide uprooted out of the sky.
Though the waters of Troublesome, of Trace Fork,
Of Sand Lick rise in a single body to glean the valleys,
To drown lush pennyroyal, to unravel rail fences;
Though the sun-ball breaks the ridges into dust
And burns its strength into the blistered rock
I cannot leave. I cannot go away.

Being of these hills, being one with the fox
Stealing into the shadows, one with the new-born foal,
The lumbering ox drawing green beech logs to mill,
One with the destined feet of man climbing and
    descending,
And one with death rising to bloom again, I cannot go.
Being of these hills I cannot pass beyond.

GLOSSARY

This glossary was designed to enlighten the reader to any dialect, nicknames, or esoteric expressions used in this text.

allus: always
bam-gilly tree: Balm of Gilead
Baptist Tower: Tower of Babel
barn (adj.): barren
Big Eyed Bird: God
Big Morning: Resurrection Day
booby owl: Barred owl
bubby: calycanthus blossom
budget: valise
bull-rag (verb): tease
carriony: (bad odor) disreputable person
cave (verb): cavil
CCC: Civilian Conservation Corps.
chewing the cud (noun): idle chatter
cork bush: hibiscus
corn night: March 31
corn planter bird: brown thrush
crackling bread: crisp browned pork skins crumbled in
    the dough
crazy head: hypertension
creeping Charlie: ground ivy
Cross Bar Hotel: county jail
dead soldier: empty whiskey bottle
dibble-dabbles: small amount
dogtick: castor bean
doughbeater: wife

flakestand: container filled with flowing water to hold the
    worm (condenser) in a moonshine still
gitworks: reproductive organs
glass window: ice
going to straw: giving birth
hame: lame
healer: faith doctor
health doctor: general practitioner appointed by the
    county
heart-leaf: leaf of wild ginger
Hell-Each-Way: Helechawa (Morgan County)
hippo: constant complainer (hypochondriac)
hit the shucks: go to bed
house: home
hypoed (adj.): inclined towards hypochondria
ice potato: Irish potato
jasper: wasp, or unworthy person
jenny barn: bootlegger joint with women of ill repute
jillion: numerous
Jockey Day: first day of Circuit Court
jubious: dubious
keeping guineas: to warn off revenuers
kilt: killed (wilted, when referring to lettuce)
knowance: knowledge
laid to my day: happened in my time
law: sheriff, constable
long-johns: long underwear
maw-maw: grandmother
Moose Hart: Wolfgang Amadeus Mozart
mort: many (mortal lot)
nitname: nickname
Old Man Thomas: Ed'nd Thomas, dulcimer maker
out of pocket: missing
pack (verb): carry
pain in cheek: tick douloureux (trigeminal neuralgia)
peckerwood: woodpecker
pick: pet, favorite
pig's chestnuts: scrotum
pippin: variety of apple
piss ant: large black ant (small black ant called *anty-mar*)
plime-blank: point blank

plum granny: (noun): Queen Ann's pocket melon
plunder: furniture
poke: sack
'possum baby: favorite
rio lamp: oil lamp with mantel wick (trade name)
Rowan tree: mountain ash (Sorbus americana)
rue back: reverse the trade
rusty: prank
sad (referring to bread dough): won't rise
sass: vegetables
sass patch: garden
saw (verb, referring to a fiddle): play
sexton peg: nail used as substitute for missing button
shanks-mare (verb): walk
sharp tack: a know-it-all
short dog bus: connecting line between Hindman and
    Vicco, Kentucky
Silver War: American Civil War, 1861–65
skewbald: mixed colors
spark (verb): court
splatter match: standing far enough apart so nobody gets
    hurt
'still: distillery
Straight Creek: brand of whiskey
sugar (as in "I've got the sugar."): diabetes
sun ball: watch
Sunday School people: missionaries
swarp: strike
tadwhacker: small boy
thrash: thrush
tide: flood
turkle: turtle
turning milk: sour
underly: underprivileged
war: feud
warmhouse: cellar
water dog: spring lizard
whang: taste
widow-man: widower
with-it: whatever else
worm tree: catalpa

BIBLIOGRAPHY

Compiled by William Terrell Cornett

1. "Nancy Hanks: A Playlet in Three Acts." Harrogate, Tenn.: Lincoln Memorial University, 1929. Unpublished. Presented at Lexington Ky., Middlesboro, Ky., and Harrogate, Tenn., May-July 1929.

2. "Place Names in the Cumberland Mountains." *American Speech* 5, no. 2 (December 1929); 113. [Article]

3. "Christian Names in the Cumberlands." *American Speech* 5, no. 4 (April 1930): 306-7. [Article]

4. "The Function of Dreams and Visions in the Middle English Romances." M.A. Thesis, Vanderbilt University, 1930. Unpublished.

5. "Dreams." *Arcadian Magazine* 1, no. 3 (April 1931): 23. [Poem]

6. "A Burned Tree Speaks." *Boy's Life* 21, no. 1 (October 1931): 61. [Poem]

7. "Horse Swapping Court." *Our Dumb Animals* 66 (January 1933): 7. [Article]

8. "Answer." *Kaleidograph* 7, no. 2 (June 1935): 13. [Poem]

9. "Mountain Dulcimer." *Virginia Quarterly Review* 11 (July 1935): 396. [Poem]. Reprinted in *Literary Digest*, 27 July 1935, p. 28; and as "Dulcimer" in *Mountain Life and Work* 39, no. 2 (Summer 1965): 15.

10. "Horse Swapping on Troublesome Creek." *Saturday Review of Literature* 12, no. 11 (13 July 1935): 10. [Poem]

11. "These Goodly Things." *The Better Home* 1, no. 3 (July-August-September 1935): 15. [Short story]

12. "Wilderness." *Kaleidograph* 7, no. 5 (September 1935: 8. [Poem]

13. "Dulcimer." *Mountain Life and Work* 11, no. 3 (October 1935): 10. [Poem]

14. "Mountain Fox Hunt." *Poetry* 47, no. 1 (October 1935): 12. Reprinted in *Literary Digest*, 5 October 1935, p. 25. [Poem]

15. "Mountain Infare." *Poetry* 47, no. 1 (October 1935): 13. [Poem]

16. "When the Dulcimers Are Gone." *Poetry* 47, no. 1 (October 1935): 14. [Poem]

17. "Mountain Twilight." *Sewanee Review* 43, no. 4 (October-December 1935): 435. [Poem]

18. "Mountain Heritage." *New Republic* 85 (18 December 1935): 170. [Poem]. Set to music by Harvey O. Davis for the Rafinesque Bicentennial Celebration, Transylvania College, Lexington, Ky., 22 October 1983. Choir directed by Harvey O. Davis.

19. "Death on the Mountain." *Mountain Life and Work*, 11, no. 4 (January 1936): 15 [Poem]

20. "Shield of the Hills." *Mountain Life and Work* 1, no. 4 (January 1936): 15. [Poem]

21. "Mountain Men: (1) Uncle Ambrose, (2) Clabe Mott." *Kaleidograph* 7, no. 9 (January 1936); 9. [Two poems]

22. "The Hill-Born." *Sewanee Review* 44, no. 1 (January-March 1936): 99. [Poem]

23. "Aftergrass." *Kaleidograph* 7, no. 10 (February 1936): 6. [Poem]

24. "Child in the Hills." *Atlantic* 157, no. 2 (February 1936): 226. [Poem]

25. "Passenger Pigeons." *New York Times*, 5 February 1936, p. 18. [Poem]

26. "Mountain Farm." *The Household* 36, no. 3 (March 1936): 58. [Poem]

27. "Fox Hunt on Defeated Creek." *Frontier and Midland* 16, no. 3 (Spring 1936): 186. [Poem]

28. "Spring Foal." *Mountain Life and Work* 13, no. 1 (April 1936): 11. Reprinted as "Foal" in *Wind* 2, no. 7 (Spring 1973): 3; and as a limited edition broadside, King Library Press, University of Kentucky, July 1982.

29. "Black Bread." *Publications of the Poetry Society of Florida*, 1936, 1 page. [Poem]

30. "On Troublesome Creek." *Sewanee Review* 44, no. 2 (April-June 1936): 163. [Poem]

31. "Interval." *The Skyline* [Colorado], 1936, 1 page. [Poem]

32. "All Their Ways Are Dark." *Atlantic* 157, no. 6 (June 1936): 708-12. [Short story]

33. "Graveyard in the Hills." *Atlantic* 158, no. 1 (July 1936): 93. [Poem]

34. "Tracks on Stone." *The Household* 36, no. 7 (July 1936): 25. [Poem]

35. "Mountain Coal Town." *Sewanee Review* 44, no. 3 (July-September 1936): 319. [Poem]

36. "Fiddlers' Convention on Troublesome Creek." *New York Herald Tribune*, 13 July 1936, in "The Conning Tower" column. [Poem]

37. "Horse Doctor." *Frontier and Midland* 17, no. 1 (Autumn 1936): 25-28. [Short story]

38. "Journey Beyond the Hills." *Yale Review* 26, no. 1 (Autumn 1936): 133.

39. "Rain on the Cumberlands." *Kaleidograph* 8 (October 1936): 9. [Poem]

40. "One Leg Gone to Judgment." *Mountain Life and Work* 12, no. 3 (October 1936): 9-10. [Short story]

41. "Dance on Pushback Mountain." *Esquire* 6, no. 4 (October 1936): 65. [Poem]

42. "A Bell on Troublesome Creek." *The Better Home* 2, no. 4 (October-November-December 1936): 3. [Short story]

43. "Death in the Forest." *Saturday Review of Literature* 14, no. 26 (24 October 1936): 4. Reprinted in *Chattahoochee Valley Times* [Lanett, Ala.], 31 January 1940, p. 4; and in *Virginia-Pilot* [Norfolk, Va.], 11 February 1940: section 1, 6. [Poem]

44. "On Defeated Creek." *Frontier and Midland* 17, no. 2 (Winter 1936–37): 120-24. [Short story]

45. "The Quare Day." *The Household* 37, no. 1 (January 1937): 36. [Short story]

46. "On Redbird Creek." *Sewanee Review* 45, no. 1 (January-March 1937): 23. [Poem]

47. "Pattern for Death." *Nation* 144, no. 1 (2 January 1937): 22. [Poem]

48. "Death on Troublesome Creek." *Kaleidograph* 8, no. 10 (February 1937): 12. [Poem]

49. "Job's Tears." *Atlantic* 159, no. 3 (March 1937): 353-58. [Short story]

50. "A Hillsman Speaks." *Arcadian Life* 24 (February 1937): 2. [Poem]

51. "Spring on Troublesome Creek." *New Republic* 80 (31 March 1937): 237. [Poem]

52. "Hounds on the Mountain." *Sewanee Review* 14, no. 2 (April-June 1937): 165. Reprinted in *Unaka Range* #4 (June 1977): 6. [Poem]

53. "Horseback in the Rain." *Frontier and Midland* 17, no. 3 (Spring 1937): 158. [Poem]

54. "With Hands like Leaves." *Kaleidograph* 8, no. 12 (April 1937): 4. [Poem]

55. "River of Earth." *Mountain Life and Work* 13, no. 1 (April 1937): 9. [Poem]

56. "White Highways." *Poetry* 50 (May 1937): 70. Reprinted in *Kentucky Alumnus* 50, no. 3 (Summer 1980): 16-17. [Poem]

57. "Earth Bread." *Poetry* 50 (May 1937): 71. [Poem]

58. *Hounds on the Mountain.* New York: Viking Press, 1937. 55 pp. Reprinted in a limited edition of 250 hardcover copies by the Anvil Press, Lexington, Ky., 1965. 55 pp. Dedication of the book changed.   Contents:
  I. Hounds on the Mountain
  "Child in the Hills" (see no. 24)
  "Mountain Dulcimer" (see no. 9)
  "Fox Hunt" [original title: "Fox Hunt on Defeated Creek"] (see no. 27)
  "Horse Swapping on Troublesome Creek" (see no. 10)
  "Infare" [original title: "Mountain Infare"] (see no. 15)
  "When the Dulcimers Are Gone" (see no. 16)
  "Journey Beyond the Hills" (see no. 38)
  "Hounds on the Mountain" (see no. 52)
  II. Creek Country
  "On Troublesome Creek" (see no. 30)
  "On Redbird Creek" (see no. 46)
  "Farm" [original title: "Mountain Farm"] (see no. 26)
  "Spring on Troublesome Creek" (see no. 51)
  "Court Day"
  "On Double Creek"
  III. Earth-Bread
  "Mountain Coal Town" (see no. 35) "Earth-Bread" (see nos. 29 and 57)
  "Night in the Coal Camps"
  IV. Death on the Mountain
  "Pattern for Death" (see no. 47)
  "Death on the Mountain" (see no. 19)
  "Graveyard" [original title: "Graveyard in the Hills"] (see no. 33)
  "Epitaph for Uncle Ira Combs, Mountain Preacher"
  "Nixie Middleton"
  "Death in the Forest" (see no. 43)
  "Come Down from the Hills"
  "Passenger Pigeons" (see no. 25)
  V. The Hill-Born
  "The Hill-Born" (see no. 22)
  "White Highways" (see no. 56)

"Rain on the Cumberlands" (see no. 39)

"Uncle Ambrose" (see no. 21)

"Eyes in the Grass"

"With Hands like Leaves" (see no. 54)

"On Buckhorn Creek"

"Horseback in the Rain" (see no. 53)

"Heritage" [original title: "Mountain Heritage"] (see no. 18)

59. "High Pastures." *Fantasy* 5, no. 4 (1937): 16. [Poem]

60. "A Man Singing to Himself" *New York Times*, 27 July 1937, p. 7. [Poem]

61. "Sun-Ball on the Mountain." *North Georgia Review* 2, no. 2 (Summer 1937): 6. Reprinted as "Now Day Has Come." *Twigs XI* 1 (Fall 1974): 105. [Poem]

62. "The Egg Tree." *Yale Review* 27, no. 1 (September 1937): 100-9. [Short story]

63. "Lost Brother." *Frontier and Midland* 18, no. 1 (Autumn 1937): 13-16. [Short story]

64. "Brother to Methusalem." *Story* 11, no. 64 (November 1937): 45-52. [Short story]

65. "Troublesome Creek Country." *Play-Actin'* 1 (November 1937): 3. [Semi-fictional descriptive article]

66. "I Shall Go Singing." *Arcadian Life* 32 (February 1938): 1. [Poem]

67. "Leap, Minnows, Leap." *Saturday Review of Literature* 17, no. 16 (12 February 1938): 5. [Poem]

68. "Mole-Bane." *Atlantic* 161, no. 3 (March 1938): 372-74. [Short story]

69. "Journey to the Settlement." *Mountain Life and Work* 14, no. 1 (April 1938): 11-13. Reprinted in *Read* 1, no. 2 (April 1941): 5-6. [Short story]

70. "Morning on the Hills." *The Better Home* 4 (April-May-June 1938): 15. [Poem]

71. "Child's Country." *New York Times*, 22 May 1938, p. K-8. [Poem]

72. "Banjo Bill Cowley." *The Household* 38, no. 7 (July 1938): 1. [Poem]

73. "Uncle Jolly." *Atlantic* 162, no. 1 (July 1938): 68-71. [Short story]

74. "Bat Flight." *Saturday Evening Post* 211, no. 10 (3 September 1938): 12-13, 50-51. [Short story]

75. "Mountain Fiddle." *The Household* 38, no. 7 (September 1938): 1. [Poem]

76. "Mountain Men Are Free." *Arcadian Life* 36 (September-October 1938): 27. Reprinted in *Fantasy* 6, no. 1 (1938): 28. [Poem]

77. "Pigeon Pie." *Frontier and Midland* 19, no. 1 (Autumn 1938): 44-45. [Short story]

78. "Book Boy on Troublesome." Broadside published by Hindman Settlement School, Hindman, Ky., ca. 1938, 1 page. [Semi-fictional descriptive piece]

79. "Hill-Lonely." *The Household* 38, no. 11 (November 1938): 1. [Poem]

80. "So Large a Thing as Seven." *Virginia Quarterly Review* 14, no. 1 (Winter 1938): 17-25. [Short story]

81. "Death in the Hills." *Fantasy* 6, no. 2 (1939): 22. [Poem]

82. "Twelve Pears Hanging High." *Mountain Life and Work* 15, no. 1 (April 1939): 14-18. [Short story]

83. "Two Eyes—Two Pennies." *Saturday Evening Post* 211 (1 April 1939): 12-13, 94-95, 97. [Short story]

84. "Sugar in the Gourd." *Prairie Schooner* 12, no. 2 (Summer 1939): 99-104. [Short story]

85. "The Ploughing." *Atlantic* 104, no. 6 (December 1939): 776-78. Reprinted in *Read Magazine* 42, no. 16 (15 April 1959): 21-23. [Short story]

86. "Death of An Old Man." *The Lyric* 17, no. 4 (Winter 1939): 183. [Poem]

87. *River of Earth.* New York: Viking Press, 1940. 245 pp. Reprinted in paperback (125 pp.) by Popular Library, New York, 1968. Some episodes from this novel appeared originally as separate stories in *Atlantic* and *Saturday Evening Post.* One section appears as a short story, "The Ploughing," in *Read Magazine* 42, no. 16 (15 April 1959): 223. Reprinted in paperback (photo-offset) by the University Press of Kentucky, Lexington, 1978. 256 pp. With a Foreword by Dean Cadle.

88. "Bloody Breathitt." *Time* 35, no. 9 (26 February 1940): 2. [Descriptive essay, quasi open letter]

89. "On Double Creek." *Saturday Evening Post* 212, no. 40 (30 March 1940): 62. Different from poem of same title in *Hounds on the Mountain.* Reprinted as "Granny Frolic on Wolfpen" in *Mountain Life and Work* 43, no. 4 (February 1968): 23. [Poem]

90. "I Love My Rooster." *Saturday Evening Post* 212, no. 40 (13 April 1940): 16-17, 62, 64, 67, 70-71. [Short story]

91. "Snail Pie." *American Mercury* 50 (June 1940): 209-14. [Short story]

92. "Death of a County Sheriff." *North Georgia Review* 5, no. 2 (Summer 1940): 6. Reprinted as "Passing of a County Sheriff" in *Mountain Life and Work* 44, no. 6 (July 1968): 17, and in *Twigs XI,* 1 (Fall 1974): 105. [Poem]

93. "The Moving." *North Georgia Review* 5, nos. 3-4

(Winter 1940–41): 18-20. Reprinted in *Wind*, 1974–76 issue, p. 87. [Short story]

94. "This Man Dying." *Fantasy* 7 (1941): 20. [Poem]

95. "The Proud Walkers." *Saturday Evening Post* 213, no. 45 (10 May 1941): 111-14. [Short story]

96. "Mountain Preacher." A concert performed at the Manhattan School of Music, New York City, 12 May 1941. Music by Ethel Glenn Hier. Lyrics by James Still. Chorus and orchestra of the Manhattan School of Music, Hugh Ross, Conductor. Included five poems from *Hounds on the Mountain* set to music: "Death on the Mountain" (see no. 19), "Epitaph for Uncle Ira Combs, Mountain Preacher," "Graveyard" (see no. 33), "Journey Beyond the Hills" (see no. 38), "When the Dulcimers Are Gone" (see no. 16).

97. "The Stir-Off." *Mountain Life and Work* 17, no. 3 (Fall 1941): 1-7. [Short story]

98. *On Troublesome Creek.* New York: Viking, 1941. 190 pp. [Short stories]   Contents:

I. Up Creek
"I Love My Rooster" (see no. 90)
"The Proud Walkers" (see no. 95)
"Locust Summer"
"The Stir-Off" (see no. 97)
"On Quicksand Creek" [original title: "Sugar in the Gourd"] (see no. 84)
"Journey to the Forks"

II. Down Creek
"Brother to Methusalem" (see no. 64)
"Snail Pie" (see no. 91)
"The Moving" (see no. 93)
"The Scrape" [original title: "On Defeated Creek"] (see no. 44)

99. "Hit Like to 'a' Killed Me." *Courier-Journal Roto-Magazine* [Louisville, Ky.], 19 April 1942, p. 22. [Humorous article]

100. [Letter to His Father]. *Chattahoochie Valley Times* [Lannet, Ala.], 3 March 1943, p. 4. [About a "bush trip" in North Africa during World War II]

101. [Letter]. *New York Herald-Tribune*, 5 November 1944, Book Review Section. [Concerns the folk song "Green Grew the Rushes, Oh"]

102. "Drought on Troublesome." *Virginia Quarterly Review* 21, no. 2 (Spring 1945): 238. [Poem]

103. "Mrs. Razor." *Atlantic* 176, no. 1 (July 1945): 52-53. Reprinted in *Statement,* Spring 1967, pp. 25-26; in *Mountain Life and Work* 30, no. 3 (Summer 1954); and in *Appalachian*

Heritage 8, no. 2 (Spring 1980): 47-49. Dramatized on Radio Tokyo by United States Army Special Services, 1947. [Short story]

104. "Cedar of Lebanon." *American Mercury* 62 (March 1946): 292-95. [Short story]

105. "Maybird Upshaw." *American Mercury* 63 (August 1946): 61-66. [Short story]

106. "Pattern of a Man." *Yale Review* 36 (Autumn 1946): 93-100. [Short story]

107. "School Butter." *Virginia Quarterly Review* 22, no. 4 (Autumn 1946): 561-69. [Short story]

108. "Apples." *Atlantic* 179, no. 2 (February 1947): 112. [Poem]

109. "The Broken Ibis." *Virginia Quarterly Review* 23, no. 3 (Summer 1947): 385. [Poem]

110. "The Nest." *Prairie Schooner* 22, no. 1 (Spring 1948): 53-56. Reprinted in *Mountain Life and Work* 44, no. 1 (November 1968), 13-16. [Short story]

111. "A Master Time." *Atlantic* 183, no. 1 (January 1949): 43-46. [Short story]

112. "A Ride on the Short Dog." *Atlantic* 188, no. 1 (July 1951): 55-58. Reprinted in *Appalachian Heritage* 2, no. 4, and 3, no. 1 (Fall-Winter 1974—75): 136-40. [Short story]

113. "The Fun Fox." *Woman's Day* 101 (September 1953); 101, 141. Reprinted in *Mountain Life and Work* 44, no. 4 (May 1968): 12-15. [Short story]

114. "Early Whippoorwill." *Nation* 178, no. 13 (17 March 1954): 263. Reprinted in *Appalachian Heritage* 2, no. 4, and 3, no. 1 (Fall-Winter 1974—75): 141. [Poem]

115. "Abandoned House." *Progressive Farmer* 69, no. 4 (April 1954): 102. [Poem]

116. "This Is My Best." *Mountain Life and Work* 30, no. 3 (Summer 1954): 32ff. [Article]

117. "Beloved Place." *Saturday Evening Post* 227 (17 July 1954): 78. Reprinted as "Littcarr, Kentucky," in *Mountain Life and Work* 42, no. 2 (Summer 1966): 21. [Poem]

118. "The Burning of the Waters." *Atlantic* 198, no. 4 (October 1956): 55-60. [Short story]

119. "Kentucky Post Office." *Courier-Journal* [Louisville, Ky.], 29 March 1957, section 2, p. 23. [Game story]

120. "The Kentucky Riddle." *Courier-Journal* [Louisville, Ky.], 4 April 1957, section 2, p. 27. [Game story]

121. "Apple Trip." *New York Times*, 17 June 1958, p. 28. Reprinted in *Mountain Life and Work* 39, no. 3 (Fall 1963): 45. [Poem]

122. "The Run for the Elbertas." *Atlantic* 204, no. 1 (July 1959): 46-53. [Short story]

123. "Litter Barrel, Kentucky." In "The Grapevine" column by Joe Creason, *Courier-Journal* [Louisville, Ky.], 5 May 1963, p. 4. [Humorous anecdote]

124. "Funnel Spider." *Appalachian Review* 2, no. 3 (Spring 1968): 14. [Poem]

125. "Encounter on Keg Branch." *Mountain Life and Work* 65, No. 2 (1969): 14-15. [Short story]

126. "The Trees in the Road." *Appalachian Review* 2, no. 2 (Winter 1968): 5. [Poem]

127. "Lamp." *Mountain Life and Work* 45, no. 4 (April 1969), special pagination. Reprinted in *Appalachian Heritage* 1, no. 1 (Winter 1973): 45. [Poem]

128. "Man O' War." *Approaches*, May 1969. [Poem]

128A. "Lizard." *Approaches* 7, no. 2 (Winter/Spring 1971): 5. [Poem]

129. "On Being Drafted into the Army from My Log Home on Wolfpen Creek in March, 1942." *Approaches* 8, no. 2 (Spring 1972): 5. [Poem]

130. "Statement to a Candidate." *Mountain Life and Work* 50, no. 12 (December 1974), back cover. [Poem]

131. *Way Down Yonder on Troublesome Creek: Appalachian Riddles and Rusties.* New York: G.P. Putnam's Sons, 1974. [53 pp.] With pictures by Janet McCaffrey. [Children's book]

132. *The Wolfpen Rusties: Appalachian Riddles and Gee-Haw Whimmy-Diddles.* New York: G.P. Putnam's Sons, 1975. [53 pp.] With pictures by Janet McCaffrey. Contains reprints of "On Wolfpen Creek" [original title: "Beloved Place"] (see no. 117); "Apple Trip" (see no. 121); "Dance on Pushback" [original title: "Dance on Pushback Mountain"] (see no. 41); and "Granny Race" [original title: "On Double Creek"] (see no. 58). [Children's book]

133. *Pattern of a Man and Other Stories.* Lexington, Ky.: Gnomon Press, 1976. 122 pp. [Short stories]   Contents:
"Mrs. Razor" (see no. 103)
"A Master Time" (see no. 111)
"Snail Pie" (see no. 91)
"A Ride on the Short Dog" (see no. 112)
"The Nest" (see no. 110)
"Pattern of a Man" (see no. 106)
"Maybird Upshaw" (see no. 105)
"Sharp Tack" [original tide: "Cedar of Lebanon"] (see no. 104)

"Brother to Methusalem" (see no. 64)

"The Scrape" [original title: "On Defeated Creek"] (see
    no. 44)

"Encounter on Keg Branch" (see no. 125)

134. "Winter Tree." *Appalachian Heritage* 4, no. 1 (Winter
1976): 60. [Poem]

135. "Welcome, Somewhat, Despite the Disorder." *Confrontations* 1, no. 2 (Spring-Summer 1977): 1. [Poem]

136. [Letter]. *Knoxville News-Sentinel,* 14 July 1977. Reprinted in *Appalachian Heritage* 7, no. 1 (Winter 1979): 58.
[Tribute to Tennessee author James Stokley]

137. *Sporty Creek: A Novel about an Appalachian Boyhood.* New York: G.P. Putnam's Sons, 1977. 125 pp. Illustrated by Janet McCaffrey. [Short stories arranged as a novel]
Contents:

"Simon Brawl" [original title: "The Ploughing"] (see no. 85)

"School Butter" (see no. 107)

"Low Glory" [original title: "I Love My Rooster"] (see no. 90)

"The Moving" (see no. 93)

"The Force Put"

"Locust Summer" [see no. 98]

"The Dumb-Bull"

"Plank Town"

"Tight Hollow" [original title: "The Burning of the Waters"]
    (see no. 118)

"Journey to the Forks" (see no. 98)

138. *Jack and the Wonder Beans.* New York: G.P. Putnam's Sons, 1977. [32 pp.]. Illustrated by Margot Tomes.
[Children's book. Retelling of "Jack and the Beanstalk"]

139. "Of the Wild Man." *The Wild Man: Touchstone* [Knoxville, Tenn.], no. 6 (Autumn 1978), no pagination. [Poem]

140. "Memorial Day: Little Carr Creek." *Kentucky Poetry Review* [James Still Issue] 14, no. 1 (Winter-Spring 1978): 4.
[Poem]

141. "Hunter." *Kentucky Poetry Review* [James Still Issue] 14, no. 1 (Winter-Spring 1978): 5. [Poem]

142. "Are You Up There, Bad Jack?" *Appalachian Heritage* 7, no. 2 (Spring 1979): 58. [Poem]

143. "Visitor." *Wind* 10, no. 38 (1980): 70. [Poem]

144. "Common Crow." *Kentucky Poetry Review* 16, nos. 2-3 (Summer-Fall 1980): 50. [Poem]

145. *The Run for the Elbertas.* Lexington: The University Press of Kentucky, 1980. 144 pp. Foreword by Cleanth Brooks.
[Short stories]   Contents:

"I Love My Rooster" (see nos. 90 and 98)

"The Proud Walkers" (see nos. 95 and 98)
"Locust Summer" (see no. 98)
"Journey to the Forks" (see no. 98)
"On Quicksand Creek" (see no. 98)
"The Stir-Off" (see nos. 97 and 98)
"The Burning of the Waters" (see nos. 118 and 137)
"School Butter" (see no. 107)
"The Moving" (see nos. 93 and 97)
"One Leg Gone to Judgment" (see no. 40)
"The Quare Day" (see no. 45)
"The Fun Fox" (see no. 113)
"The Run for the Elbertas" (see no. 122)

146. *River of Earth: The Poem and Other Poems.* Lexington, Ky.: Workshop of the King Library Press, 1982–83. [15 pp.] Includes "James Still: An Appreciation," by Edward F. Prichard, Jr. and an afterword by John B. Stephenson. Printed in a limited edition (65 numbered copies). Contents:
"River of Earth" (see no. 55)
"Now Day Has Come" (see no. 61)
"Morning" [original title: "Morning on the Hills"] (see
    no. 70)
"A Child's Wisdom" [original title: "Child's Country"] (see
    no. 71)
"The Trees in the Road" (see no. 126)
"Of the Wild Man" (see no. 139)
"Aftergrass" (see no. 23)
"Lamp" (see no. 127)
"Wolfpen Creek" [original title: "Beloved Place"] (see
    nos. 117 and 132)
"Banjo Bill Brewer" [original title: "Banjo Bill Cowley"] (see
    no. 72)
"Hunter" (see no. 141)
"Memorial Day: Little Carr Creek" (see no. 140)
"Passing of a County Sheriff" (see no. 92)
"Clabe Mott" (see no. 21)
"After Some Twenty Years Attempting to Describe a Flow-
    ering Branch of a Redbud" (written for this volume)

147. "Ballad." *Appalachian Heritage* 11, no. 3 (Summer 1983): 3. [Poem]

148. "On the Passing of My Brother Alfred." *Kentucky Poetry Review* 20, no. 2 (Fall 1984): 108. [Poem]

149. "What Have You Heard Lately?" *New Letters* 51, no. 2 (Winter 1984–85): 38. [Poem]

150. "Madly to Learn." *New Letters* 51, no. 2 (Winter 1984–85): 38-39. [Poem]

151A. "High Field." *Appalachian Heritage* 13, nos. 1-2 (Winter/Spring 1985): 15. [Poem]

151B. "Unemployed Coal Miners" and "Here In My Bed." *Kentucky Poetry Review* 21, no. 1 (Spring/Summer 1985): 29. [Poems]

151. *The Wolfpen Poems.* Berea, Ky.: Berea College Press, 1986. 82 pp. [Poems]   Contents:

I. Troublesome Creek
"Leap Minnows, Leap" (see no. 67)
"Drought" [original title: "Drought on Troublesome"] (see no. 102)
"Farm" [original title: "Mountain Farm"] (see nos. 26 and 58)
"Hounds on the Mountain" (see no. 52)
"Buckhorn Creek" (see no. 58)
"Pattern for Death" (see nos. 47 and 58)
"Rain on the Cumberlands" (see no. 39)
"The Hill-born" (see nos. 22 and 58)
"Court Day" (see no. 58)
"Redbird Creek" (see nos. 46 and 58)
"Come Down from the Hills" (see no. 58)
"Graveyard" [original title: "Graveyard in the Hills"] (see nos. 33 and 58)
"Now Has Day Come" (see no. 61)
"Dance on Pushback" (see no. 41)
"Funnel Spider" (see no. 124)
"Dulcimer" (see nos. 9, 13, and 58)
"River of Earth" (see no. 55)
"Troublesome Creek" (see nos. 30 and 58)
"Year of the Pigeons"

II. Little Carr Creek
"Child in the Hills" (see no. 24)
"Spring"
"Infare" [original title: "Mountain Infare"] (see nos. 15 and 58)
"Horse Swapping" (see no. 10)
"Fox Hunt" (see nos. 14 and 58)
"Clabe Mott" (see no. 21)
"White Highways" (see nos. 56 and 58)
"I Was Born Humble" [original title: "Death in the Forest"] (see nos. 43 and 58)
"Nixie Middleton" (see no. 58)
"Epitaph for Uncle Ira Combs, Mountain Preacher" (see nos. 58 and 96)

"Banjo Bill Brewer" [original title: "Banjo Bill Cowley"]
(see nos. 72, 146)
"Earth-bread" (see nos. 57 and 58)
"Night in the Coal Camps" (see no. 58)
"Mountain Coal Town" (see nos. 35 and 58)
"Journey Beyond the Hills" (see no. 58)
"Uncle Ambrose" (see nos. 21 and 58)
"Death on the Mountain" (see nos. 19 and 58)
"Passing of a County Sheriff" [original title: "Death of a
County Sheriff"] (see no. 92)
"On Double Creek" (see no. 58)
"Ballad" (see no. 147)
"Aftergrass" (see no. 23)
"Memorial Day: Little Carr Creek" (see no. 140)
III. Wolfpen Creek
"The Broken Ibis" (see no. 109)
"Lamp" (see no. 127)
"Eyes in the Grass" (see no. 58)
"The Common Crow" (see no. 133)
"With Hands Like Leaves" (see nos. 54 and 58)
"When the Dulcimers Are Gone" (see nos. 16 and 58)
"The Trees in the Road" (see no. 126)
"Apple Trip" (see no. 121)
"Apples" (see no. 108)
"Early Whippoorwill" (see no. 114)
"On Being Drafted into the U.S. Army from My Log
Home in March 1942" (see no. 129)
"Are You Up There, Bad Jack?" (see no. 142)
"Granny Frolic" [original title: "On Double Creek"] (see
no. 89)
"Lizard" (see no. 129)
"Morning: Dead Mare Branch" [original title: "Morning
on the Hills"] (see nos. 70 and 146)
"Wolfpen Creek" (see no. 117)
"Statement to a Candidate" (see no. 130)
"Foal" [original title: "Spring Foal"] (see no. 28)
"Horseback in the Rain" (see nos. 53 and 58)
"Hunter" (see no. 141)
"Death of a Fox"
"Passenger Pigeons" (see nos. 25 and 58)
"A Child's Wisdom" [original title: "Child's Country"]
(see nos. 71 and 146)
"Winter Tree" (see no. 134)
"Of the Wild Man" (see no. 139)

"High Field" (see no. 151A)

"Heritage" [original title: "Mountain Heritage"] (see nos. 18 and 58)

152. "In My Dreaming." *Kentucky Poetry Review* 23, no. 2 (Summer/Fall 1987): 48. [Poem]

153. "Yesterday in Belize." *Kentucky Poetry Review* 24, no. 2 (Fall 1988): 6. [Poem]

154. *Rusties and Riddles and Gee-Haw Whimmy-Diddles.* The University Press of Kentucky, 1989. Pictures by Janet McCaffery. [112 pages] A reprinting of *Way Down Yonder on Troublesome Creek* (see no. 131) and *The Wolfpen Rusties* (see no. 132).

155. "Artist." *Kentucky Poetry Review* 25, no. 2 (Fall/Winter 1989/90): 102. [Poem]

156. "Heritage." *The Country Traveler.* New York: Time-Life, 1990, 82. (see no. 18)

157. "Those I Want In Heaven With Me Should There Be Such a Place." *Appalachian Journal* 18, no. 2 (Winter 1991): 222. [Poem]

Note: For their assistance in preparing this bibliography, I would like to thank Faye Belcher and Wilma Howard of Morehead State University and Sidney Farr of Berea College. I would especially like to thank Dr. Joseph Bryant, Albert Stewart, Dr. Robert Denham, and, of course, James Still.

William Terrell Cornett
Southeast Community College
Cumberland, Kentuky

Reprinted from *Iron Mountain Review* 2, no. 1 (Summer 1984): 29-33, by permission of Mr. Cornett and the publishers. Additions and corrections by Mr. Cornett and James Still.

"That man who's single on Dead Mare Branch, they say he's got books stacked from the floor to the ceiling. My opinion, he owns many volumes of devilish writing."